NW

CLASSIC GANGSTER FILMS

CLASSIC GANGSTER FILMS

ROBERT BOOKBINDER

A Citadel Press Book
Published by Carol Publishing Group

TO MY PARENTS

ACKNOWLEDGMENTS

Warner Brothers, United Artists, 20th Century-Fox,
Universal Pictures, Paramount Pictures, M.G.M.,
R.K.O., Allied Artists, Columbia Pictures, American-
International Pictures; special thanks to Paula Klaw
of Movie Star News and Mark Ricci of The Memory
Shop for help in gathering the stills for this book.

Carol Publishing Group Edition - 1993

A Citadel Press Book
Published by Carol Publishing Group
Citadel Press is a registered trademark of Carol Communications, Inc.

Editorial Offices: 600 Madison Avenue, New York, NY 10022
Sales & Distribution Offices: 120 Enterprise Avenue, Secaucus, NJ 07094
In Canada: Canadian Manda Group, P.O. Box 920, Station U
Toronto, Ontario, M8Z 5P9, Canada
Queries regarding rights and permissions should be addressed to:
Carol Publishing Group, 600 Madison Avenue, New York, NY 10022

Designed by A. Christopher Simon
Manufactured in the United States of America
IBN 0-8065-1467-1

10 9 8 7 6 5 4 3 2 1

Carol Publishing Group books are available at special discounts
for bulk purchases, for sales promotions, fund raising, or
educational purposes. Special editions can also be created to
specifications. For details contact: Special Sales Department,
Carol Publishing Group, 120 Enterprise Ave., Secaucus, NJ 07094

Library of Congress Cataloging in Publication Data

Bookbinder, Robert.
    Classic gangster films.
    1. Gangster films--United States--Plots,
themes, etc. I. Title
PN1995.9.G3B66 1985 791.43'09'09355 84-27434

CONTENTS

INTRODUCTION

The gangster film has always been one of the staples of the American cinema. Like the horror film, the western and the musical, gangster movies have never failed to fascinate the public, and the genre continues to be popular to this day, thanks to such major contemporary film-makers as Francis Ford Coppola and Brian De Palma who, with their stunning productions of *The Godfather* (1971), *The Godfather, Part II* (1974) and the 1983 remake of *Scarface,* are keeping the genre alive and well more than fifty years after its beginnings.

Though the record shows that there were several motion pictures with a gangster theme produced as far back as the silent era, the genre did not really begin to flourish as a popular form

until the thirties, when it reigned throughout the decade as one of the public's favorite kinds of "escapist" entertainment. Depression-era audiences responded strongly to all the action, violence and romance that these films contained, and were more than willing to get caught up in the colorful on-screen exploits of Edward G. Robinson, James Cagney and Humphrey Bogart as a means of temporarily easing the pain and frustration of bad economic times. In a sense, the movie gangster, with his rebellious breaking of society's rules and regulations, and his aggressive drive to "get somewhere" regardless of consequences, became something of a hero to filmgoers of the period. The tough, uncompromising way in which Robinson, Cagney and Bogart handled any situation was no doubt admired by the average citizen, who might have liked to emulate such behavior as a means of lashing out against economic oppression, but who would never have the courage or conviction to do so.

The boom period of the gangster film lasted from 1930 to 1942 and, during that time, nearly all the major studios tried their hands at producing pictures of this type, often with excellent results, but none ever managed to match the staggering output of Warner Brothers, who churned out something like 40 vintage crime thrillers (of both the class "A" and "B" quality) during this period, all of which became box office successes.

Not surprisingly, the gangster cinema produced its share of superstars who, due to their many appearances in these films, became identified with them throughout their entire careers, and were never able to escape the tough guy image despite the fact that they graduated to important roles in non-gangster movies. Edward G. Robinson, James Cagney and Humphrey Bogart are, even today, the three actors most associated with films of this type, which isn't surprising, since all three achieved their initial fame in a Warner Brothers crime drama, and each went on to appear in at least a dozen more during their tenures at the studio.

With the arrival of the forties, Robinson, Cagney and Bogart purposefully sought to escape from the gangster mold and move on to other things, leaving the way clear for an entire new generation of screen actors who, because of their tough, combative images, became briefly associated with the genre. Stars like Alan Ladd, John Garfield and Kirk Douglas appeared in several gangster pictures that were well produced and splendidly acted, but which did not, as was hoped, generate a new cycle of crime films. As a result, the output of gangster movies during the forties was considerably less than it had been the decade before, and it was evident from the handful that were produced that the genre was undergoing a period of major transition.

The lawless but basically sympathetic characters of the Robinson-Cagney-Bogart era were, more and more, being replaced by sadistic and often psychotic screen criminals who generated genuine fear in audiences. Three of the most

memorable characters of the era—Richard Widmark's Tommy Udo in *Kiss of Death* (1947), James Cagney's Cody Jarrett in *White Heat* (1949) and Everett Sloane's Albert Mendoza in *The Enforcer* (1951)—were a far cry from earlier screen hoods, who were usually depicted as men from "the wrong side of the tracks" who turned to crime as a means of escaping poverty. This new breed were inherently demented and evil men, who truly seemed to enjoy their trade, especially when it involved murder and mayhem.

The movies themselves also grew increasingly harsh and realistic in their physical presentation, and the beautiful high contrast black-and-white photography that had graced many crime dramas of the thirties was being replaced by a pale, bland type of monochrome that strongly resembled the kind used in documentary films. In addition, the use of studio sets, which had been a Hollywood tradition since the twenties, was also, for the most part, being discontinued. Instead, the gangster pictures of this era were shot on actual locations, which gave the films a greater feeling of reality.

The years stretching from the fifties to the early seventies saw, in addition to these grimmer and more downbeat films, a spate of "biographical" gangster epics, which explored the lives of well-known real-life criminals whom most audiences had read about in newspapers and books. Among the famous gangsters to get the full film treatment were Al Capone, John Dillinger, Joseph Valachi, and Bonnie Parker and Clyde Barrow. During the early seventies, the crime picture was given a revival of sorts with the release of Francis Ford Coppola's epic Mafia tales *The Godfather* and *The Godfather, Part II,* which became the most successful gangster movies ever made. Ten years later, the genre got an additional shot in the arm with the 1983 premiere of Brian De Palma's epic reworking of the classic 1932 film *Scarface,* which, despite some of the most graphic and bloody scenes in gangster movie history, managed to attract audiences by the millions and become one of the year's largest grossing films. Though the production of gangster pictures may never again be as active as it was during the glory days of Warner Brothers, it is safe to assume that they will continue to entertain moviegoers for many years to come.

LITTLE CAESAR

A WARNER BROTHERS–VITAPHONE PICTURE.   1930

Edward G. Robinson and Sidney Blackmer

CREDITS

Directed by Mervyn Leroy; *Produced by* Hal B. Wallis; *Screenplay by* Francis Edward Faragoh; *From the novel by* W. R. Burnett; *Director of photography:* Tony Gaudio; *Film editor:* Ray Curtiss; *Art direction:* Anton Grot; *Music by* Erno Rapee; *Running time:* 77 minutes.

CAST

Rico: Edward G. Robinson; *Joe Massara:* Douglas Fairbanks, Jr.; *Flaherty:* Thomas Jackson; *Olga:* Glenda Farrell; *Sam Vettori:* Stanley Fields; *Big Boy:* Sidney Blackmer; *Otero:* George E. Stone; *Diamond Pete Montana:* Ralph Ince; *Arnie Lorch:* Maurice Black; *Tony:* William Collier, Jr..

Little Caesar was the first of the great gangster films and, after more than fifty years, remains one of the best. It made a star of Edward G. Robinson, who had been working in films since 1923, and it laid the groundwork for all the fine Warner Brothers gangster movies that followed. Based on the hard-hitting novel by W. R. Burnett, it told of the rise and fall of a small-time hood, a character based in part on real-life gangster Al Capone, and the corrupting effect he has on everything he touches until he is finally brought to justice.

9

Douglas Fairbanks, Jr.
and Edward G. Robinson

Edward G. Robinson and Douglas Fairbanks, Jr.

Robinson, who had been a distinguished character actor on the stage before coming to Hollywood, suited the role perfectly, imbuing his definitive gangster with the snarling, pugnacious mannerisms that, perhaps to his dismay, became associated with the star for the remainder of his life. The supporting cast contained some of the legendary character actors of the era—Ralph Ince, George E. Stone, Thomas Jackson, Stanley Fields and Sidney Blackmer. The romantic subplot involving Douglas Fairbanks, Jr., and Glenda Farrell was wisely downplayed, never once getting in the way of the superbly staged gangland sequences.

Little Caesar is famous for some of the most memorable scenes in gangster movie history, such as the film's opening, in which Robinson pours out his criminal ambitions to an enraptured Fairbanks while they enjoy "spaghetti and coffee for two" at a seamy, run-down diner. In a later scene, Stanley Fields, appearing as the gangster chief who gives Robinson his first job, introduces him to "the boys," telling them, "I want you all to meet a new guy what's gonna be with us," after which the camera zooms in for a series of closeups, giving the audience a rather unnerving introduction to the evil-looking killers who make up Fields's gang.

10

Surprisingly, *Little Caesar* has hardly dated at all, and Robinson's last line (the classic "Mother of mercy . . . can this be the end of Rico?"), delivered in a weak, quivering voice as he lies dying after being ripped to shreds by police machine guns, still packs a wallop. The photography of Tony Gaudio is perhaps the finest on any of the early thirties gangster epics. Gaudio shot the picture in a rich, silvery black-and-white that gave *Little Caesar* a lavishness that the other films of the period, such as *The Public Enemy* and *Smart Money,* were lacking.

Edward G. Robinson and Adrian Morris

SYNOPSIS

Caesar Enrico Bandello (Robinson), a petty thug, dreams of becoming a major-league gangster. On their way to the big city, Rico and his young sidekick Joe Massara (Douglas Fairbanks,

Edward G. Robinson (*c*)

Jr.) stop at a small roadside restaurant and, during their meal, Bandello reveals his overwhelming ambition to become an underworld kingpin. Arriving in town, Rico manages to worm his way into the gang of racketeer Sam Vettori (Stanley Fields), beginning his career as a bodyguard and triggerman. His brilliant, fearless performance during several jobs earns Rico a promotion, and it isn't long before he becomes Vettori's right-hand man.

The police, under the leadership of Lt. Tom Flaherty (Thomas Jackson), begin a running war with Vettori and his mob, and the pressures of having to deal with both the cops and rival gangs take their toll on the aging gangleader. The hard-as-nails Rico, completely without fear and confidant he can handle whatever comes along, tells his boss, "Sam, you're getting soft. . . . You're getting so you can dish it out but you can't take it."

Not surprisingly, Rico succeeds Sam as the gang's leader not long afterward. Bandello quickly rises to the top, becoming the number one gang-ster in town, and he gives his friend Joe Massara a position of prominence in his organization. When Joe falls in love with the beautiful Olga Strassoff (Glenda Farrell), however, he decides to "go straight" and quit the rackets. Meanwhile, Rico's boys, becoming fearful that their boss's penchant for cold-blooded murder will be their undoing, overthrow Bandello.

Blackballed in the rackets by the criminal higher ups of the city, Rico sinks lower and lower, and is eventually reduced to living in a flop-house for transients. Wanting to close the file on Rico forever, Lt. Flaherty lures him out of hiding, and the gangster is killed in a shootout with police.

Little Caesar's smashing impact on the movie-going public prompted Warners to release a similar picture less than a year later. That film, *The Public Enemy*, equalled the success of *Little Caesar* and paved the way for an entire cycle of Warner Brothers gangster movies.

THE PUBLIC ENEMY

A WARNER BROTHERS–VITAPHONE PICTURE.   1931

James Cagney and Edward Woods

CREDITS

Directed by William A. Wellman; *Screenplay by* Kubec Glasmon and John Bright; *Adaptation and dialogue by* Harvey Thew; *Based on an original story by* John Bright; *Director of photography:* Dev Jennings; *Film editor:* Ed McCormick; *Art direction:* Max Parker; *Costumes by* Earl Luick; *Musical director:* David Mendoza; *Make-up by* Perc Westmore; *Running time:* 84 minutes.

CAST

Tom Powers: James Cagney; *Gwen Allen:* Jean Harlow; *Matt Doyle:* Edward Woods; *Mamie:* Joan Blondell; *Kitty:* Mae Clarke; *Ma Powers:* Beryl Mercer; *Mike:* Donald Cook; *Jane:* Mia Marvin; *Nails Nathan:* Leslie Fenton; *Paddy Ryan:* Robert Emmett O'Conner; *Putty Nose:* Murray Kinnell; *Molly:* Rita Flynn; *Mug:* Charles Sullivan.

Warner Brothers' second gangster film of the thirties was *The Public Enemy*, the film that made a star of James Cagney. It was a tougher, more realistic crime picture than its predecessor, featuring stronger scenes of violence and a more gruesome death for its gangster protagonist. By the same token, the muted, grainy images of Dev Jennings photography were a far cry from the

13

beautiful black-and-white employed in *Little Caesar*, and the settings in *The Public Enemy* all had a rather gritty, realistic quality. Unlike the later gangster films produced by Warners, *The Public Enemy* was made before the rigid censorship laws of the Hays office went into effect, and director William Wellman was free to make the picture as sexy and violent as he pleased.

Though seldom is a character actually killed on screen, the gangland murders in *The Public Enemy* (such as Cagney's point-blank blasting of Putty Nose, the small-time crook who had been his boyhood mentor in the ways of crime, and his horrific shooting slaughter of a rival gang at the film's conclusion) are far more potent than similar scenes in *Angels With Dirty Faces* (1938) and *The Roaring Twenties* (1939). Cagney's final shootout with the enemy gang must certainly rank among the most bloodcurdling scenes in gangster movie history, as the heavily armed Cagney walks into a poolhall hideout from a rain-swept street and then, seconds later, the audience hears a barrage of pistol fire followed by the agonized moans of the wounded and dying. Also, *The Public Enemy* was remarkably candid in its approach to sex, and the scenes involving Cagney and his shapely blond mistress (played by Jean Harlow) contained a

Jean Harlow, Edward Woods, James Cagney

Beryl Mercer and James Cagney

14

Mae Clarke and James Cagney

heavy erotic undercurrent never again seen in a gangster film until the release of *Bonnie and Clyde* over thirty years later.

The Public Enemy is also of special interest in that it represents one of the few times that Cagney played a completely villainous character. Whereas such later Cagney gangsters as Rocky Sullivan in *Angels With Dirty Faces* and Eddie Bartlett in *The Roaring Twenties* enlisted a great deal of audience sympathy, his Tom Powers in *The Public Enemy* was a murderous criminal utterly void of any tender human feeling. Despite this, however, moviegoers (especially women) remained fascinated by Tom Powers, whose sexual magnetism was undeniable. In addition to Cagney's superb portrayal, *The Public Enemy* was rife with excellent supporting performances, and the fine vignettes played by Joan Blondell, Jean Harlow, Beryl Mercer, Robert Emmett O'Connor, and especially Murray Kinnell as the Fagin-like Putty Nose, added greatly to making it one of the true classics of the genre.

SYNOPSIS

Tom Powers (Cagney), a policeman's son, and his friend Matt Doyle (Edward Woods), become criminals to escape the drudgery of life in the lower classes. Graduating from small-time heists to major racketeering, Tom and Matt become two of the most feared criminals in New York, and soon find themselves engaging in war with rival gangs. They join forces with Paddy Ryan (Robert Emmett O'Conner), who operates a lucrative bootlegging racket, and gradually become wealthy men from their underworld activities.

Later, Matt and Tom meet Maimie (Joan Blondell) and Kitty (Mae Clarke), two attractive young women, who become their mistresses. Though Matt eventually marries Maimie, the restless Tom grows tired of Kitty, and he leaves her for a flashy blonde named Gwen Allen (Jean Harlow).

When Matt is shot to death by an enemy gang, Tom vows to take revenge and, arming himself with two large .38 revolvers, he storms the gang's hideout and engages the mobsters in a furious gun battle. Managing to kill or seriously wound most of his enemies, Tom is badly hurt as well, and collapses in the street from his injuries. He is

James Cagney, Joan Blondell, Edward Woods

taken to the emergency hospital and recovers, but the surviving members of the rival mob sneak into his room and kidnap the weakened Tom. After killing him, they bind him grotesquely with gauze and butcher paper, and deliver Powers' bloodied corpse to his mother's doorstep.

Few actors have had a more impressive star debut than James Cagney in *The Public Enemy*, and his virtuoso portrayal took both audiences and critics completely by storm. His Tom Powers was a masterful characterization, and it launched Cagney into one of the most celebrated careers in movie history.

Edward Woods, James Cagney, Beryl Mercer

Edward Woods, Murray Kinnel, James Cagney

SMART MONEY

A WARNER BROTHERS–VITAPHONE PICTURE.   1931

Edward G. Robinson and James Cagney

CREDITS

Directed by Alfred E. Green; *Screenplay by* Kubec Glasmon and John Bright; *Based on an original story by* Lucien Hubbard and Joseph Jackson; *Additional dialogue by* Lucien Hubbard and Joseph Jackson; *Director of Photography:* Robert Kurrle; *Film editor:* Jack Killifer; *Musical direction:* Leo F. Forbstein; *Make-up by* Perc Westmore; *Running time:* 83 minutes.

CAST

Nick: Edward G. Robinson; *Jack:* James Cagney; *Irene:* Evelyn Knapp; *Marie:* Noel Francis;

District Attorney: Morgan Wallace; *Greek Barber:* Maurice Black; *D. A.'s Girl:* Margaret Livingston; *Phil:* Edwin Argus; *Sport Williams:* Boris Karloff; *Sleepy Sam:* Ralf Harolde.

With the success of *Little Caesar* and *The Public Enemy,* Warners took the next logical step by casting Edward G. Robinson and James Cagney in the same movie. While *Smart Money,* released several months after *The Public Enemy,* is a stylish, entertaining picture, it can't help but be something of a letdown to Robinson–Cagney fans, and one wonders why the studio refrained from tailoring a big-budget, action-packed gangster epic

Edward G. Robinson and James Cagney

for the two instead of casting them in this modest little crime drama, which turned out to be the only picture they ever made together.

Though, admittedly, it is enjoyable seeing Robinson and Cagney in the same movie, their roles in *Smart Money* aren't very evenly matched, and the film gave Robinson a juicy star part while inexplicably sticking Cagney with a rather color- less supporting role that, one imagines, could have been played by any one of a dozen young contract players on the Warner Brothers roster. Rumor has it that the studio, eager to capitalize on the suc- cess of *Caesar* and *Enemy* but fearing that a real blood and guts shoot-em-up starring Robinson and Cagney might prove too similar to their earlier hits, fashioned *Smart Money* to be considerably tamer. What little violence there was in the picture was brief and quickly cut away from, and the studio even injected a little lighthearted comedy into the proceedings.

The characters played by Robinson and Cagney

James Cagney, Edward G. Robinson, Charlotte Merriam

were, likewise, a far cry from the ruthless, power mad criminals Rico and Tom Powers, and were merely a pair of amiable con-men who run a crooked gambling joint. However, what *Smart Money* may have lacked in thrills and dramatic impact was more than made up for by its truly flavorful atmosphere and settings, especially the tiny gambling den in the back of Robinson's barber shop and the colorful bowery saloons the boys often frequent. Another factor in the picture's favor is that it gave Robinson and Cagney several splendid scenes together, and their final confrontation, in which Robinson suspects that Cagney has betrayed him, showed both stars off to best advantage.

The film also benefited from a brief cameo appearance by the soon-to-be famous Boris Karloff, playing a crooked gambler who is barred from Robinson's joint after he is caught cheating. Karloff was only months away from attaining international stardom in *Frankenstein*, and it is

Edward G. Robinson, Noel Francis, James Cagney

Billy House *(1c)* Edward G. Robinson, Harry Semels, James Cagney

19

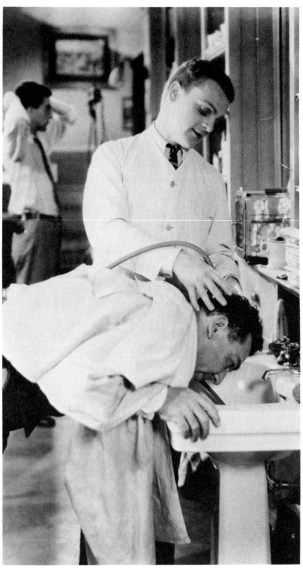

James Cagney

indeed fascinating to watch the actor in one of the last bit roles he ever played.

SYNOPSIS

New York City. Nick (Robinson), a neighborhood barber who has a weakness for whiskey and blondes, runs an illegal gambling den with the help of his young protégé Jack (Cagney). Though his profits are handsome, Nick yearns to try his gambling skills in a big-time poker game uptown, and, armed with the knowledge and skill of a lifetime, he journeys to a swank Manhattan hotel, where he buys his way into a high-stakes professional game. Finding that his opponents are no match for him, Nick wins a huge sum of money, but is cheated out of it by a cute little hotel clerk he makes a date with. Unable to get back into the game on credit, Nick returns home, where he resumes his back room gambling operation. Later, Nick finds that Jack's latest girlfriend is really an informant for the cops, hired to find out all she can about Nick's racket. Confronting Jack with what he has learned, Nick is relieved when Jack swears he knew nothing about it. Sometime later, however, Nick is arrested by the police.

Robinson delivered his customary excellent performance as Nick the Barber, the good-hearted con-man who is repeatedly played for a chump himself, and he gave his character a tinge of poignancy that made the brash little racketeer likable to audiences.

Edward G. Robinson and James Cagney

SCARFACE

A UNITED ARTISTS PICTURE.   1932

Paul Muni and Ann Dvorak

CREDITS

Directed by Howard Hawks. *Produced by* Howard Hughes. *Screenplay by* Seton I. Miller, John Lee Mahin and W. R. Burnett. *Directors of Photography:* Lee Garmes and L. W. O'Connell. *Based on the novel by* Armitage Trail. *Story by* Ben Hecht. *Film editor:* Edward Curtiss. *Music directors:* Adolph Tandler and Gus Arnheim. *Running time:* 91 minutes.

CAST

Tony Camonte: Paul Muni; *Cesca:* Ann Dvorak; *Johnny Lovo:* Osgood Perkins; *Poppy:* Karen Morley; *Gaffney:* Boris Karloff; *Rinaldo:* George Raft; *Guardino:* C. Henry Gordan; *Angelo:* Vince Barnett; *Publisher:* Purnell Pratt; *Mrs. Camonte:* Inez Palange; *Louis Costillo:* Harry Vegar; *Chief Detective:* Edwin Maxwell; *Managing Editor:* Tully Marshall; *Pietro:* Henry Armetta.

The original 1932 production of *Scarface*, released by United Artists, ranks as one of the best non-Warners gangster pictures of the thirties. Like *Little Caesar*, it was inspired in part by the sensational career of Al Capone, but unlike the earlier film, it contained scenes that were virtual recreations of incidents that actually took place in

21

George Raft, Vince Barnett,
Paul Muni, Osgood Perkins

Paul Muni and C. Henry Gordon

Capone's life, such as the murder of aging rackets boss "Big Jim" Colosimo, the St. Valentine's Day Massacre and the killing of Capone's arch enemy Dion O'Banion in the latter's flower shop. *Scarface* was released in March of 1932 to generally excellent reviews, although some of the edge had unfortunately been taken off the picture by the earlier premieres of *Little Caesar* and *The Public Enemy.*

The acting in *Scarface,* especially that of Paul Muni and George Raft, was superlative, and it remains the most graphically violent gangster movie of its day. Interestingly, Howard Hawks spent a total of six months filming it (an inordinately long shooting schedule for a picture made during the thirties) and initially had great difficulty getting it released because the censorship board insisted that he tone down some of the more brutal scenes and make the Paul Muni character less sympathetic. Also, they insisted that Hawks film an alternate ending in which Muni, shot by police in the original version, would instead be hanged for his crimes. Complying with the censors, Hawks reedited *Scarface* and went through the enormous trouble and expense of shooting another ending, but, incredibly, the board still wasn't satisfied with the results and failed to pass it again. However, the battle between Hawks and the censors finally simmered down sometime later and *Scarface* was finally released, although the heavy editing the director was forced to do marred the picture's continuity, and one can only speculate on what a truly magnificent film it must have been before Hawks was ordered to cut it.

Scarface is notable, among other reasons, as the first film in which George Raft did his famous coin-tossing bit, which became the actor's trademark; and also for the casting of Boris Karloff, fresh from his triumph in *Frankenstein,* as a British gangster who is gunned down in a crowded bowling alley. Surprisingly, most critics of the day felt that Karloff's English accent seemed out of place in an American gangster picture, repeating a similar criticism they had voiced the previous year, when Karloff appeared briefly in the Robinson–Cagney film, *Smart Money.* Despite this, however, Karloff, with his piercing eyes and ability to project

Paul Muni and Ann Dvorak

23

menace, was a definite asset to both films, and his well-acted scenes in *Scarface* remain among the movie's high points.

SYNOPSIS

The story takes place in Chicago. Racketeer Johnny Lovo (Osgood Perkins), seeking to corner the market on bootlegged liquor, hires an ambitious young hood named Tony Camonte (Muni) to wipe out the competition. "Big Louis" (Harry Vegar), Lovo's aging boss, who is getting soft, has become more of a liability than an asset, and Johnny orders Camonte to bump him off. Becoming Lovo's second-in-command after murdering "Big Louis," Tony cuts a swift and bloody path to the top, and he engineers the massacre of an entire rival gang at a bowling alley.

Seeking to seize Lovo's power, Tony romances Johnny's mistress, Fluff (Karen Morley). Fearful that the power-hungry young thug might displace him, Lovo orders Tony killed. However, when Lovo's men try to take him for a ride, the clever Tony escapes and, in retaliation, he orders his friend Rinaldo (Raft) to kill Lovo. With Johnny out of the way, Camonte becomes the most powerful gangleader in Chicago, but complications arise when his sister Cesca (Ann Dvorak) falls in love with Rinaldo. Enraged when they begin an affair, Tony kills Rinaldo, after which Cesca reports the murder to the police. The cops storm the gangster's hideout and kill Tony, who collapses under an electric sign advertising the slogan "The World at Your Feet."

Scarface was largely responsible for launching the careers of Muni and Raft, whose appearances in the film made them two of the hottest actors of the year. Following the premiere of *Scarface,* Muni began a long and fruitful association with Warner Brothers which did not, surprisingly enough, include a single gangster role, and Raft was placed under a seven-year contract to Paramount.

LADY KILLER

A WARNER BROTHERS–VITAPHONE PICTURE.   1933

Mae Clarke and James Cagney

CREDITS

Directed by Roy Del Ruth. *Screenplay by* Ben Markson. *Director of Photography:* Tony Gaudio. *Art direction:* Robert Haas. *Film editor:* George Amy. *Musical conductor:* Leo F. Forbstein. *Production supervisor:* Henry Blanke. *Costumes by* Orry-Kelly. *Assistant director:* Chuck Hansen. *Make-up by* Perc Westmore. *Running time:* 76 minutes.

CAST

Don Quigley: James Cagney; *Myra Gale:* Mae Clarke; *Lois Underwood:* Margaret Lindsay; *Duke:* Leslie Fenton; *Ramick:* Henry O'Neill; *Conroy:* Willard Robertson; *Smiley:* Russell Hopton; *Williams:* William Davidson; *Brannigan:* Robert Elliott; *Kendall:* John Marston; *Spade Maddock:* Douglas Dumbrille; *Thompson:* George Chandler; *Butler:* Olaf Hytten.

Smart Money, Warner Brothers' "follow-up" to *Little Caesar* and *The Public Enemy,* had been more of a vehicle for Robinson than for Cagney, which was no doubt a disappointment to many of the actor's fans. Cagney's role in the picture had been minor, to say the least, and it allowed him to display none of the tough arrogance and vitality

Margaret Lindsay, James Cagney

James Cagney, Douglas Dumbrille, Mae Clarke, Russell Hopton, Leslie Fenton

which had become his trademark ever since *The Public Enemy*. Though the studio had definitely slighted Cagney in *Smart Money*, they more than made up for it the following year, and cast the star in the kind of roughhouse gangster picture that was decidedly more suited to his talents.

The film was called, appropriately enough, *Lady Killer*, and it reunited Cagney with his co-star from *The Public Enemy*, Mae Clarke. Their "assault and battery romance" in the earlier movie (during which Clarke had received the famous grapefruit in the face) had proved enormously popular with audiences, and *Lady Killer* again cast Clarke as a nagging mistress whom Cagney periodically belts around to keep in line. Surprisingly enough, the studio and the stars managed to top the grapefruit bit with the superbly choreographed scene in which Cagney grabs the screaming Clarke by the hair, yanks her clear across the room and then tosses her out the door, giving her a swift kick in the backside as she exits.

Though obviously an attempt to recreate some of the feel of *The Public Enemy*, *Lady Killer* was a terrific little gangster picture in its own right,

containing the usual melodramatic goings-on but also spicing up the proceedings with equal parts of comedy and Hollywood satire (in this sense, *Lady Killer* was a prelude to the first full-fledged gangster comedy, *Jimmy the Gent*, released the following year). The script by Ben Markson pretty much followed the standard Warners crime movie formula, only this time combined it with the then-popular trend of giving the audience a behind-the-scenes look at Hollywood.

Lady Killer featured Cagney as a small-time racketeer who, through a fateful chain of events, becomes a movie star, and there were several amusing scenes in which Cagney was seen playing various screen roles, including an Indian chief and a young nobleman. As a nice contrast, the gangster sequences were played straight, giving *Lady Killer* a balance of comedy and seriousness that was quite refreshing.

SYNOPSIS

The plot, such as it was, revolved around an ambitious young tough guy named Don Quigley

(Cagney) who, after being fired from his job as a movie usher, decides to embark on a life of crime in an effort to advance himself. He assembles a gang of colorful thugs and, after engineering a series of lucrative swindles, becomes a front-ranking mobster. Later, however, the cops are tipped off to his activities and try to arrest Don, forcing the young crook to leave town. He heads West, finally landing in Hollywood, where, as fate would have it, he manages to land a bit role in a movie. Through a crazy chain of events, Don becomes a top romantic idol, and takes the glamorous Myra Gale (Mae Clarke) for his mistress. Their relationship soon sours, however, and Don ends up throwing her out of his apartment bodily. Back in New York, his old gang learns of Don's fame, and they rush to Hollywood, where they try to persuade Don to resume his criminal career.

In addition to Mae Clarke, Margaret Lindsay was also seen to good advantage in *Lady Killer,* appearing as a movie actress whom Cagney tries to romance.

James Cagney and William Davidson *(in sweater)*

JIMMY THE GENT

A WARNER BROTHERS–VITAPHONE PICTURE.   1934

Allen Jenkins, James Cagney, Bette Davis

CREDITS

Directed by Michael Curtiz. *Executive producer:* Jack L. Warner. *Screenplay by* Bertram Millhauser. *Based on an original story by* Laird Doyle, Ray Nazarro. *Director of photography:* Ira Morgan. *Art direction:* Esdras Hartley. *Dialogue director:* Daniel Reed. *Film editor:* Thomas Richards. *Musical conductor:* Leo F. Forbstein. *Make-up by* Perc Westmore. *Costumes by* Orry-Kelly. *Running time:* 67 minutes.

CAST

Jimmy Corrigan: James Cagney; *Joan Martin:* Bette Davis; *Mabel:* Alice White; *Louie:* Allen Jenkins; *Joe:* Arthur Hohl; *James J. Wallingham:* Alan Dinehart; *Ronnie Gatston:* Phillip Reed; *The Imposter:* Hobart Cavanaugh; *Gladys:* Mayo Methot; *Hendrickson:* Ralf Harolde; *Mike:* Joseph Sawyer; *Posy:* Nora Lane; *Judge:* Joseph Crehan.

Like the western and the horror film, the gangster genre produced its share of comedies, tongue-in-cheek spoofs depicting the racketeers as rather likable fellows who seemed to have a great deal of fun living outside the law. There was seldom any violence or gunplay in these gangster comedies, and the idea of a character getting killed or seriously hurt in the story was practically taboo. Not surprisingly, the stars of these lighthearted

Bette Davis and James Cagney

crime pictures were, more often than not, the three great stars of the genre—Edward G. Robinson, James Cagney and Humphrey Bogart—each of whom had several of these gangster romps to his credit. Rumor has it that the three actors truly enjoyed appearing in these pictures, relishing the challenge of having to make audiences laugh, and the change of pace from the often somber and humorless characters they played in their straight gangster pictures.

Jimmy the Gent, produced by Warners in 1934 and starring James Cagney and Bette Davis, was the original gangster comedy and remains one of the very best. It was a well-scripted, no-holds-barred satire of the genre, directed with style and flair by Michael Curtiz and featuring Cagney in a non-stop, high-intensity comic performance that was, in many ways, a forerunner to his unforgettable work in Billy Wilder's *One Two Three* nearly thirty years later. Bette Davis, also appearing in a rare comic fling, was almost equally impressive as Cagney's wisecracking girl Friday. And Allen Jenkins, who appeared in many gangster comedies over the years and came to specialize in them, was hilarious as Cagney's amiable but slow-witted sidekick (he played similar roles in two of Edward

G. Robinson's best known comedies, *Brother Orchid* and *Larceny, Inc.*, released in the early forties).

Jimmy the Gent was an immediate hit with audiences, proving that the genre lent itself well to this sort of kidding around, and that the movie-going public thoroughly enjoyed watching stars like Cagney poke fun at their images. Not surprisingly, Warners produced several more gangster comedies during the succeeding years, but none managed to capture the spirit and zest of *Jimmy the Gent*.

SYNOPSIS

Gangster Jimmy Corrigan (Cagney) runs a profitable inheritance racket, in which he seeks out unclaimed fortunes and provides fake beneficiaries. The flashy racketeer is in constant competition with the stuffy, conservative James J. Wallingham (Alan Dinehart), who runs the same kind of crooked operation but who, unlike Jimmy, puts on airs of respectability. Jimmy's girlfriend and assistant, Joan Martin (Bette Davis), tired of being an accessory to Corrigan's swindles, leaves him to work for Wallingham, claiming that he is both honest and a "gentleman who prefers the finer things in life," something the street-tough Jimmy is not. In an effort to win Joan back, Jimmy visits Wallingham's plush offices one afternoon, hoping that some of his competitor's culture and refinement might rub off on him. Later on, Jimmy tells his sidekicks Louie (Jenkins) and Joe (Arthur Hohl) that he has decided to turn over a new leaf and become a gentleman. Somewhere down the line, however, Jimmy learns that Wallingham is, in reality, shadier than he himself ever was. Exposing the pompous fraud and agreeing to "mend his ways and go legit," Jimmy persuades Joan to come back to him.

Cagney's superb flair for comedy was evident throughout *Jimmy the Gent,* and Warners later cast the performer in a string of non-gangster comedies as well. Always one of Hollywood's most respected serious actors, Cagney proved in all these films that he was equally brilliant at light-weight material.

30

G-MEN

A WARNER BROTHERS PICTURE.   1935

Russell Hopton, James Cagney, Edward Pawley, Barton MacLane

CREDITS

Directed by William Keighley. *Screenplay by* Seton I. Miller. *Director of photography:* Sol Polito. *Art direction:* John J. Hughes. *Film editor:* Jack Killifer. *Musical director:* Leo F. Forbstein. *Costumes by* Orry-Kelly. *Make-up by* Perc Westmore. *Running Time:* 85 minutes.

CAST

James "Brick" Davis: James Cagney; *Kay McCord:* Margaret Lindsay; *Jean Morgan:* Ann Dvorak; *Jeff McCord:* Robert Armstrong; *Brad Collins:* Barton MacLane; *Hugh Farrell:* Lloyd Nolan; *McKay:* William Harrigan; *Danny:* Edward Pawley; *Eddie:* Regis Toomey; *Kratz:* Edwin Maxwell; *Bruce Gregory:* Addison Richards; *Venke:* Harold Huber; *The Man:* Raymond Hatton.

By 1935, James Cagney had become one of Hollywood's top box office attractions and one of Warner Brothers' highest-paid stars, commanding a salary of $4,500 per week. Throughout the thirties, the studio, in an effort to display his versatility, featured Cagney in many different kinds of movies, and the actor proved that he was just as adept at musicals and light comedies as he was at crime pictures. It was, however, in gangster

James Cagney and Robert Armstrong

movies that audiences liked Cagney best, and most of his films produced during this period were of that genre. At mid-decade, however, the studio came up with a truly unique idea . . . they would cast perrenial bad guy Cagney in a gangster film that would place him on the right side of the law for a change.

Dusting off an old story property called, somewhat ironically, *Public Enemy Number One,* the studio fashioned a vehicle in which Cagney would fight the forces of gangland evil as a two-fisted member of the newly formed Federal Bureau of Investigation. The studio realized the box office potency of casting Cagney in this kind of role, and gave the picture an avalanche of publicity playing up the fact that the screen's favorite badman was doing a complete turnabout, and would be playing, for the first time, a crime-fighting crusader. Interestingly, many of the pressbooks for *G-Men,*

Robert Armstrong, James Cagney, Edward Pawley

32

issued shortly before the picture's release, featured two comparison photos of the star—one a shadowy portrait of the snarling Tom Powers from *The Public Enemy* and the other a shot of the refined, clean-cut young lawman he was playing in *G-Men*.

Shot in just six weeks on a budget of $450,000, the film, with its clever publicity campaign and offbeat casting of Cagney, was a whopping box office success, opening to rave critical reviews and standing-room-only crowds. Some of the notices referred to *G-Men* as Cagney's best film since the original *The Public Enemy*, which, in many ways, it was. And though the star was playing a crime fighter in the picture, he retained the tough, pugnacious attitude that had served him so well in gangster roles, making his character doubly threatening to lawbreakers. The direction of *G-Men* was entrusted to William Keighley, one of Warners' top directors of the thirties, and one of

Robert Armstrong, James Cagney

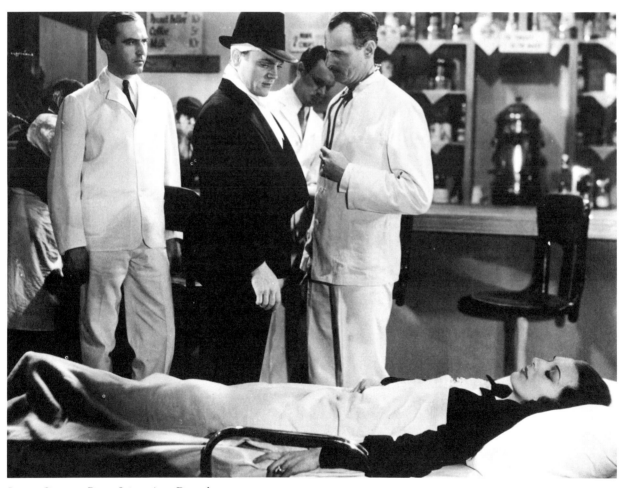

James Cagney, Perry Ivins, Ann Dvorak

James Cagney and Ann Dvorak

Ann Dvorak and James Cagney

Cagney's favorite co-workers (interestingly, following the success of *G-Men,* the studio planned to feature Cagney in a large-scale Technicolor adaptation of *Robin Hood,* to be directed by Keighley, but the project never materialized).

SYNOPSIS

G-Men cast Cagney as Brick Davis, a young lawyer who, despite his intelligence and skill, cannot seem to get his practice off the ground. Once a slum kid with little hope for the future, Davis had been blessed by an extraordinary stroke of good luck as a child, when he was practically

adopted by a wealthy rackets boss (William Harrigan), who gave the boy a decent home and put him through law school. Now growing weary of his fruitless legal career and seeking a more exciting profession, Brick joins the Federal Bureau of Investigation. His training at the FBI Academy is long and arduous, made even more so by the fact that his instructor, a laconic wiseguy named Jeff McCord (Robert Armstrong), doesn't like him.

When Brick's best friend Eddie Buchanan (Regis Toomey) is murdered by gangsters, Davis vows to avenge his death. Meanwhile, Brick falls in love with McCord's sister Kay (Margaret Lindsay) and, in an effort to learn the identities of the hoods who killed Eddie, Brick questions his

old girlfriend Jean (Ann Dvorak), whose husband has connections in the criminal underworld. Still in love with Brick, Jean worms the information out of her husband and relays it to Davis, who later kills his friend's murderers in a bloody shootout.

In addition to its original 1935 release, *G-Men* was also reissued in 1949 to coincide with the FBI's 25th Anniversary. Interestingly, a newly shot prologue was tacked on to the re-release prints, in which David Brian appeared as a bureau chief addressing a classroom full of rookies, telling them that they (and the audience) are about to see the "grand-daddy" of all FBI pictures.

THE PETRIFIED FOREST

A WARNER BROTHERS PICTURE.   1936

Bette Davis and Leslie Howard

CREDITS

Directed by Archie Mayo. *Screenplay by* Charles Kenyon and Delmer Daves. *Based on the play by* Robert E. Sherwood. *Associate producer:* Henry Blanke. *Director of photography:* Sol Polito. *Music:* Bernard Kaun. *Film editor:* Owen Marks. *Art director:* John Hughes. *Assistant director:* Dick Mayberry. *Gowns by* Orry-Kelly. *Sound recording by* Charles Lang. *Running time:* 83 minutes.

CAST

Alan Squier: Leslie Howard; *Gabrielle Maple:* Bette Davis; *Duke Mantee:* Humphrey Bogart; *Mrs. Chisholm:* Genevieve Tobin; *Boze:* Dick Foran; *Jackie:* Joseph Sawyer; *Mr. Chisholm:* Paul Harvey; *Gramp Maple:* Charley Grapewin; *Ruby:* Adrian Morris; *Slim:* Slim Thompson.

Humphrey Bogart had been a sensation in the 1935 Broadway production of *The Petrified Forest*. The actor's portrayal of Duke Mantee, the hunted gangster who, while taking refuge at a small roadside café, discovers a kindred spirit in the unlikely form of a sensitive, troubled writer, was masterful in every respect, but he wasn't even considered for the part when Warner Brothers

36

secured the movie rights. The studio felt that, despite his success with the stage version, Bogart was still a relatively unknown commodity to movie audiences, despite the fact that he had been working in pictures, on and off, since 1930.

Warners assembled a sterling cast to bring Robert E. Sherwood's drama to the screen, including Leslie Howard (who would repeat his stage role), Bette Davis, Dick Foran, Joseph Sawyer and Charley Grapewin, and, not surprisingly, the studio decided to play up the gangster angle of the drama by casting one of their top box office attractions, Edward G. Robinson, in the role of Mantee. Leslie Howard, however, realizing that the compelling on-stage rapport between him and Bogart had been one of the best things about the Broadway version, insisted that his old co-star be signed, and even threatened to resign from the project unless the studio complied. Since Warners rightly realized that no other actor could equal Howard's brilliance in the role of the disillusioned

poet Alan Squier, they agreed to the star's demand, and Robinson was dropped in favor of Bogart.

The film, released in 1936, received critical raves and Bogart, after years of obscurity, at last received the recognition so long overdue him. While the picture established Bogart as a front-ranking screen actor, it did not, curiously enough, make him a star, and he spent the next few years playing second fiddle to Robinson and Cagney before finally achieving stardom in *High Sierra* (1941). Sherwood's poetic, ethereal dialogue for Alan Squier, which Howard had delivered so movingly on the stage, was retained for the film version, making *The Petrified Forest* one of the most faithful stage adaptations of the period.

Though Howard's recreation of his stage role was excellent, the lion's share of critical attention went to Bogart, who very nearly stole the picture. Bogart's performance in the film was stunning, capturing the brutish mannerisms of the hoodlum with supreme skill, and making the weary gang-

Leslie Howard, Dick Foran, Bette Davis, Humphrey Bogart

Bette Davis and Leslie Howard

ster, who looks strangely forward to his date with death, seem sympathetic to the audience.

SYNOPSIS

The story takes place in the Arizona desert. Alan Squier (Howard), a sensitive writer disillusioned by the modern world, has ventured there to escape from civilization. Believing himself to be, in his words, "one of the vanishing breed of intellectuals," Squier feels painfully out of place in contemporary society, which he regards as unfeeling and violent. He is irresistably drawn to the stony mesas and haunting winds of the desert, which he feels might help quiet his troubled mind. At one point in his journey, he stops at a small roadside diner, where he meets Gabrielle (Bette Davis), a young waitress with artistic aspirations not unlike those

Humphrey Bogart
and Leslie Howard

38

he once had. She tells Alan that her greatest dream is to someday study art in France, and she shows him a few examples of her work. Drawn to each other, Alan and Gabrielle fall in love, much to the dismay of her crusty grandfather (Charley Grapewin).

Meanwhile, gangster Duke Mantee (Bogart), who is wanted dead or alive by the authorities, decides to hide out at the café with his "boys," and holds Alan, Gabrielle, the old man, and several other people hostage. During his stay at the small restaurant, Mantee forms a strange kinship with Squier, arising out of the fact that both men are, in a sense, adrift in a hostile, uncaring world in which they clearly do not belong. Sometime afterward, Squier makes Gabrielle the beneficiary of his $5,000 life insurance policy and, realizing that the money would make it possible for her to

Humphrey Bogart, Leslie Howard, Bette Davis

Humphrey Bogart, Bette Davis, Leslie Howard, Dick Foran, Slim Thompson, Joseph Sawyer, director Archie Mayo (*seated center*) and Charley Grapewin

39

Charley Grapewin, Genevieve Tobin, Leslie Howard, Paul Harvey, Bette
Davis, Slim Thompson, Humphrey Bogart, Joseph Sawyer

realize her dream, he asks Duke to kill him sometime before the gangster leaves. As Mantee prepares to depart later on, Alan reminds him of his promise, after which the criminal guns the writer down, killing him. Not long after Mantee and his gang make a break for it, they are apprehended by police.

Some twenty years after the film version, Bogart played Mantee again in a television adaptation of *The Petrified Forest,* in which the parts of Alan and Gabrielle were played by Henry Fonda and Lauren Bacall.

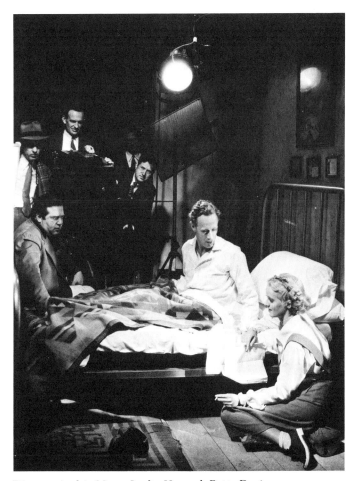

Director Archie Mayo, Leslie Howard, Bette Davis

41

BULLETS OR BALLOTS

A WARNER BROTHERS PICTURE.   1936

Edward G. Robinson and Humphrey Bogart

CREDITS

Directed by William Keighley. *Screenplay by* Seton I. Miller. *Based on an original story by* Martin Mooney and Seton I. Miller. *Associate producer:* Louis F. Edelman. *Director of photography:* Hal Mohr. *Film editor:* Jack Killifer. *Music by* Heinz Roemheld. *Art direction:* Carl Jules Weyl. *Assistant director:* Chuck Hansen. *Sound recording by* Oliver S. Garretson. *Running time:* 81 minutes.

CAST

Johnny Blake: Edward G. Robinson; *Lee Morgan:* Joan Blondell; *Nick "Bugs" Fenner:* Humphrey Bogart; *Al Kruger:* Barton MacLane; *Herman:* Frank McHugh; *Captain McClaren:* Joseph King; *Driscoll:* Richard Purcell; *Wires:* George E. Stone; *Bryant:* Henry O'Neill.

Though Edward G. Robinson was teamed with James Cagney only once, he co-starred with Warners' other major gangster star—Humphrey Bogart—in four crime epics between 1936 and 1940. It is, in a way, somewhat ironic that Bogart became such a frequent co-star of Robinson's, since it was he who had replaced the more established actor as arch-criminal Duke Mantee in 1936's *The Petrified Forest*. The Robinson–Bogart

Frank McHugh, Humphrey Bogart, Joan Blondell

films—*Bullets or Ballots* (1936), *Kid Galahad* (1937), *The Amazing Dr. Clitterhouse* (1938) and *Brother Orchid* (1940)—were really star vehicles for Robinson with Bogart lending support, always appearing as the villian of the piece. The first, *Bullets or Ballots,* had the advantage of being made right on the heels of *The Petrified Forest,* and benefited from having not only the popular Robinson in it but Bogart as well, who now also had a measure of box office clout as a result of his acclaimed portrayal of Mantee.

 Bullets or Ballots gave Bogart little to do except lurk menacingly in the background, while the film provided Robinson with an actor's field day. Appearing as an honest cop who pretends to join the rackets in the hope of busting them from the inside, Robinson was excellent in his mini-tour-de-force, and he made Johnny Blake a far more complex character than was usually seen in films of this kind. Robinson had the difficult task of making the character appear to be acting the part of a dishonored cop turned thug, which made the role of Blake doubly challenging. Robinson was, of

Humphrey Bogart, Barton MacLane, Edward G. Robinson

Humphrey Bogart and Edward G. Robinson

course, more than equal to the task, delivering a finely shaded performance as the law officer ordered to undertake a dangerous and difficult assignment.

Perhaps the most memorable scene in *Bullets or Ballots* was the shootout between Bogart and Robinson toward the end of the story, when Robinson's undercover scheme is exposed and Bogart attempts to gun him down. This scene was well handled by director William Keighley, who employed skillful quick-cutting techniques to make the gun battle of the two stars more furious and exciting. *Bullets or Ballots* also featured an especially enjoyable performance from favorite Warners tough guy Barton MacLane, appearing as the gangster chief who masterminds the rackets.

SYNOPSIS

The criminal empire of Al Kruger (MacLane) is flourishing in New York City, thanks to a corrupt political administration and the financial help of three anonymous bankers, whose identity is known only to Kruger. Bryant (Henry O'Neill), an honest, crime-fighting newspaper editor, is murdered before he can expose the rackets, and a grand jury hires the toughest cop in the city— Captain Dan McLaren (Joseph King)—to wage an all-out war against the syndicate. Sometime later, Johnny Blake (Robinson), a respected plainclothes officer, is suddenly fired from the force for misconduct, and begins looking for a more lucrative profession. The embittered ex-cop befriends Kruger and is later hired as one of the gangster's chief lieutenants, much to the dismay of Kruger's second-in-command, Nick "Bugs" Fenner (Bogart). Blake, actually doing an undercover assignment for McLaren, begins learning all the intricate workings of the rackets, and starts relaying his findings to McLaren on a weekly basis.

A series of devastating police raids on various mob strongholds follows, forcing Kruger to consider other avenues of criminal endeavor. Blake suggests that the mob should take over the profitable numbers racket, which accounts for more illegal revenue in New York than all the other rackets combined. When Blake's suggestion subsequently makes millions for the mob, Fenner begins fearing that the former policeman might take his place as Kruger's right-hand man. Seeking to take over all the rackets himself, Fenner kills Kruger, fully expecting to be named his successor. As it turns out, however, the leadership of the syndicate is inherited by Blake, who finally learns the identities of the bankers who are at the financial center of it all. Before he can relay this information to McLaren, though, Blake is fingered as a police spy and Fenner forces him into a deadly gun battle, during which both men are seriously wounded. Fenner dies from his injuries, but Blake lives long enough to tell McLaren the names of the three bankers, who are subsequently arrested.

Bullets or Ballots benefited from a certain topicality in that it attempted to deal with the problem of crime in high places. In this instance, the real villains of the piece were not the gangsters played by Bogart and MacLane, but rather the corrupt political machine and the three bankers who enabled the rackets to flourish while masquerading as respected citizens.

KID GALAHAD

A WARNER BROTHERS PICTURE.   1937

William Haade, Humphrey Bogart, Ben Welden

CREDITS

Directed by Michael Curtiz. *Screenplay by* Seton I. Miller. *Based on a novel* by Francis Wallace. *Associate producer:* Samuel Bischoff. *Director of photography:* Tony Gaudio. *Film editor:* George Amy. *Music by* Max Steiner and Heinz Roemheld. *Dialogue director:* Irving Rapper. *Art direction:* Carl Jules Weyl. *Gowns by* Orry-Kelly. *Assistant director:* Jack Sullivan. *Sound recording:* Charles Lang. *Running time:* 101 minutes.

CAST

Nick Donati: Edward G. Robinson; *Fluff:* Bette Davis; *Turkey Morgan:* Humphrey Bogart; *Ward Guisenberry:* Wayne Morris; *Marie Donati:* Jane Bryan; *Silver Jackson:* Harry Carey; *Chuck McGraw:* William Haade; *Joe Taylor:* Joe Cunningham; *Buzz:* Ben Welden; *Barney:* Frank Faylen; *Sam:* Bob Evans.

By far the best of the Robinson Bogart films, *Kid Galahad* remains one of the most carefully produced Warners gangster pictures of the thirties. The studio seemed to go all out this time around, giving it a larger than average budget and elaborate production values that rank it, at least technically, alongside *Angels With Dirty Faces* and *The Roaring Twenties.* The unusually rich black-and-white photography of Tony Gaudio, with its

46

excellent use of shadows to heighten the atmosphere, was a definite plus factor, as were a full-blooded musical score by Max Steiner and the appearance, in addition to Robinson and Bogart, of another Warner favorite, Bette Davis, in the female lead. Also in the picture's favor was its superb direction by Michael Curtiz, who kept the drama moving at an almost ferocious pace, making certain that *Kid Galahad* did not have a weak or sluggish moment in its entire length.

The story was set against the world of professional boxing, which, curiously enough, had never before served as the background in a Warner Brothers gangster saga, and Curtiz's love of the sport and the sometimes seedy environment that goes with it is evident throughout *Kid Galahad*. There are superbly conceived shots of smoke-filled fight arenas and seamy backrooms where the promoters and managers confer, and there is also some of the fiercest and most excitingly staged

Edward G. Robinson and Bette Davis

Bette Davis, Edward G. Robinson and Harry Carey

Edward G. Robinson and Bette Davis

ring footage in cinema history. The final bout between Wayne Morris and William Haade remains unmatched for brutal realism, as Morris is mercilessly pounded around the ring by Haade's devastating punches.

The film was cast to perfection, with Bette Davis appearing at her most beguiling and sexy as Robinson's mistress and Wayne Morris likably innocent as the young fighter trapped in a corrupt game and seeking a way out. Likewise, William Haade, a massive, mean-looking actor in the Bruce Cabot vein, presented a truly fearsome figure as the champion who is managed by the big-time gangster played by Bogart. This time out, Robinson portrayed a wholly sympathetic character as the small-time fight manager who dreams of molding a champion.

Harry Carey, Humphrey Bogart, Bette Davis, Ben Welden, Wayne Morris, Edward G. Robinson

Harry Carey, Wayne Morris, Humphrey Bogart, Edward G. Robinson, William Haade

Like the boxing sequences, the gunfights in *Kid Galahad* were also staged by Curtiz for stark realism, and the picture gave Robinson and Bogart their second great screen shootout. *Kid Galahad* was, in many ways, a textbook example of how a gangster film should look and feel. The excellent sets were designed by Carl Jules Weyl, one of the studio's top art directors, who also engineered the splendid sets for *The Adventures of Robin Hood*. The many convincing backgrounds used in *Kid Galahad* (like the elegantly decadent club where Bogart and Robinson meet to talk business) added greatly to the picture's atmosphere and mood.

SYNOPSIS

Nick Donati (Robinson), a fight manager whose greatest wish is to someday have a champion, finds a lively prospect in Ward Guisenberry (Wayne Morris), a bellhop who KO's boxing champion Chuck McGraw (William Haade) in a hotel brawl. Signing Ward up immediately, Nick puts him on a rigorous training program under the guidance of veteran trainer Silver Jackson (Harry Carey). Nicknamed Kid Galahad by Donati's mistress Fluff (Bette Davis), Ward becomes a top-ranking contender, and later falls in love with Nick's sister Marie (Jane Bryan). When Nick learns that Fluff has fallen for the young boxer herself, he becomes jealous and arranges for Galahad to meet the champ, hoping that a solid beating will deflate the Kid's ego. He sets the bout up with Turkey Morgan (Bogart), McGraw's gangster-manager, and, certain that Galahad won't stand a chance in a real championship fight, Nick bets against him, assuring Morgan that the Kid won't last three rounds.

Familiar with McGraw's murderous, mauling style of boxing, Nick intentionally gives Galahad the wrong strategy before the fight, telling him to slug it out with the champ. As a result, the Kid takes a horrible beating for seven rounds. However, when Marie and Fluff plead with Nick to stop the carnage, he has a change of heart and gives Galahad the proper instructions—to evade the champ's punches by moving around the ring, and to jab McGraw at every opportunity. Following this advice, Galahad wears McGraw down and finally KO's him. Realizing he has been double-crossed by Nick, Morgan storms Galahad's dressing room after the fight and, in a furious exchange of gunfire, both the gangster and Nick are killed. Fed up with the corrupt fight game and yearning for a cleaner life, Galahad quits while still champion, and marries Marie.

Kid Galahad contained a truly colorful performance from Harry Carey as the crusty trainer who fashions Galahad into a contender. In 1962 the story was reworked into, of all things, a musical vehicle for Elvis Presley.

Harry Carey, Humphrey Bogart, William Haade, Edward G. Robinson, Ben Welden

DEAD END

A SAMUEL GOLDWYN PRODUCTION.   1937

Billy Halop, Bobby Jordan, Leo Gorcey, Huntz Hall, Gabe Dell, Bernard Punsley

CREDITS

Released through United Artists. *Directed by* William Wyler. *Produced by* Samuel Goldwyn. *Screenplay by* Lillian Hellman. *Based on the play by* Sidney Kingsley. *Director of photography:* Gregg Toland. *Film editor:* Daniel Mandell. *Art direction:* Richard Day. *Set decorations:* Julia Heron. *Costumes by* Omar Kiam. *Special effects by* James Basevi. *Running time:* 93 minutes.

CAST

Drina: Sylvia Sidney; *Dave:* Joel McCrea; *Baby Face Martin:* Humphrey Bogart; *Kay:* Wendy Barrie; *Francey:* Claire Trevor; *Hunk:* Allen Jenkins; *Tommy:* Billy Halop; *Spit:* Leo Gorcey; *T. B.:* Gabe Dell; *Dippy:* Huntz Hall; *Angel:* Bobby Jordan; *Milty:* Bernard Punsley; *Mrs. Martin:* Marjorie Main.

As a superb transfer of a stage work to the screen, the Samuel Goldwyn production of *Dead End* has few equals. The play by Sidney Kingsley, a one-set masterwork dealing with the anguish and triumphs of a group of people living in a New York slum, had been the Broadway sensation of 1936. The film version, released the following year, could hardly miss being a success, as Samuel

Sylvia Sidney and Billy Halop

aware that their charisma had been one of the main reasons for the play's success, Goldwyn wisely recruited all six of the actors to repeat their roles in the movie.

The photography for the film was handled by one of the great masters of the black-and-white camera, Gregg Toland (who later worked with Orson Welles on both *Citizen Kane* and *The Magnificent Ambersons*), who created for *Dead End*, with his brilliant use of lighting and deep-focus techniques, a series of stunning images that give the film an almost three-dimensional quality. However, perhaps the one element in *Dead End* that audiences remembered best was the magnificent set on which the story takes place, a dark maze of slum dwellings winding endlessly into the background, and dwarfed by the towering skyscrapers of Manhattan.

SYNOPSIS

The story takes place in New York City, in a slum located on the banks of the East River, where

Goldwyn studios, the owner of the movie rights, assembled a formidable cadre of talent to bring it to the screen. William Wyler, always acknowledged as one of Hollywood's master filmmakers, was hired to direct, and the screenplay was entrusted to one of the finest playwrights of the era, Lillian Hellman. Joel McCrea and Sylvia Sidney who, at that time, were both solid box office names, were assigned the romantic leads, while Goldwyn shrewdly borrowed popular bad guy Humphrey Bogart from Warners to play the lead gangster, Baby Face Martin.

The key roles in the drama were, however, those of the adolescent gang who inhabit the slum, a group of tough, street-wise young men who survive by their wits, and for whom petty crime has become a way of life. These roles had been beautifully written by Kingsley and superbly acted in the stage version by Billy Halop, Leo Gorcey, Huntz Hall, Bobby Jordan, Gabriel Dell and Bernard Punsley, who captivated Broadway with their excellent ensemble playing. The young performers worked splendidly as a unit, and, well

Sylvia Sidney and Joel McCrea

Joel McCrea

the wanted killer and berates him for "taking the easy way out."

Meanwhile, Tommy and his gang abduct Phillip Griswold (Charles Peck), a millionaire's son, and rob him of his watch, rings and wallet. When the boy's father learns what has happened, he tries to physically restrain Tommy until the police can be called, but the young hoodlum breaks free by stabbing Griswold in the arm. Though injured only slightly by this, Mr. Griswold files a complaint with the police, and gives them a detailed description of Tommy. In the meantime, Martin visits his mother and finds that she has been utterly shattered by the direction his life has taken. He also goes to see his old girlfriend Francey (Claire Trevor), and discovers that she has turned to prostitution. Disillusioned by his experiences with

a gang of teen-aged kids—Tommy (Billy Halop), Dippy (Huntz Hall), Angel (Bobby Jordan), T. B. (Gabe Dell), Milty (Bernard Punsley) and Spit (Leo Gorcey)—spend their days plotting petty crimes and jeering at the rich "swells" who inhabit a posh apartment building overlooking the slum. Onto the scene comes Baby Face Martin (Bogart), who grew up in the neighborhood years before, and who escaped *his* poverty by becoming a criminal. Now a full-fledged gangster with the murders of eight men behind him, Martin has returned to visit the haunts of his youth, and to see his aging mother (Marjorie Main). Dave Arnold (McCrea), a hard-working architect trying to get out of the slums the honest way, recognizes

Joel McCrea, Humphrey Bogart, Allen Jenkins

Francey and his mother, Martin plots the kidnapping of Phillip so that his homecoming won't be a total loss. When Dave sees Martin again, he gets into a fight with him and is pushed into the river by the gangster. Pulling himself up onto one of the docks, Dave gets into a tussel with Martin's accomplice, Hunk (Allen Jenkins), and knocks him out, stealing his revolver. Martin flees the scene with Dave in hot pursuit, and the whole impoverished community watches as Dave chases the criminal through the slum, finally cornering and killing him on a fire-escape. As a crowd gathers around Martin's body, Dave is told by police that he is due a financial reward for shooting Martin.

Spit, one of the kids in Tommy's gang, rats on Tommy to the police. Hearing of this, Tommy wrestles Spit to the ground and threatens to leave the "mark of the squealer" on him with a knife, but Dave and Tommy's sister Drina (Sylvia Sidney) intervene and talk the boy out of it. Minutes later, Tommy is spotted by Mr. Griswold and arrested by officer Mulligan (James Burke), but Dave tells Drina not to worry, as his reward money will allow them to hire a good lawyer for the boy's defense.

Interestingly, Warners was apparently so impressed by *Dead End* that they signed Billy Halop, Leo Gorcey, Huntz Hall, Bobby Jordan, Gabe Dell and Bernard Punsley to lucrative long-term contracts, and the boys went on to enliven several Warners gangster pictures, in which they were always billed as the Dead End Kids.

Humphrey Bogart and unidentified players

ANGELS WITH DIRTY FACES

A WARNER BROTHERS PICTURE.   1938

Bernard Punsley, Bobby Jordan, Billy Halop, James Cagney, Leo Gorcey, Huntz Hall, Gabe Dell

CREDITS

Directed by Michael Curtiz. *Screenplay by* John Wexley and Warren Duff. *Based on an original story by* Rowland Brown. *Director of photography:* Sol Polito. *Associate producer:* Samuel Bischoff. *Music by* Max Steiner. *Film editor:* Owen Marks. *Assistant director:* Sherry Shourds. *Art direction:* Robert Haas. *Gowns by* Orry-Kelly. *Dialogue director:* Jo Graham. *Sound recording by* Everett A. Brown. *Running time:* 97 minutes.

CAST

Rocky Sullivan: James Cagney; *Jerry Connolly:* Pat O'Brien; *James Frazier:* Humphrey Bogart; *Laury Martin:* Ann Sheridan; *Mac Keefer:* George Bancroft; *Soapy:* Billy Halop; *Swing:* Bobby Jordan; *Bim:* Leo Gorcey; *Pasty:* Gabe Dell; *Crab:* Huntz Hall; *Hunky:* Bernard Punsley; *Young Rocky:* Frankie Burke; *Edwards:* Ed Pawley.

Angels With Dirty Faces is in many ways the apex of the Warners gangster cycle, containing perhaps the finest script, direction and musical score of all the studio's classic crime pictures. It featured James Cagney in one of his most memorable performances of the thirties (for which he received an Academy Award nomination) and is

Huntz Hall, Bernard Punsley, Leo Gorcey, Bobby Jordan, Billy Halop

today remembered as the one vehicle, above all others, that epitomized the Cagney screen image . . . that of the tough but basically decent man from the wrong side of the tracks who becomes a criminal and yet is allowed to redeem himself before the final fade-out. Though his splendid work did not garner Cagney the Oscar, it did manage to win him the prestigious *New York Times* Film Critics Award, making him the first performer in history to merit a top acting honor for his portrayal of a gangster. The film reteamed

Cagney with Pat O'Brien, one of his most frequent co-stars of the thirties, and with Michael Curtiz, the studio's premier director who, three years before, had guided Cagney through the whirlwind gangster comedy *Jimmy the Gent*.

The role of Rocky Sullivan allowed Cagney to, once again, create a gangster character who succeeds in winning the sympathy of the audience despite his lawlessness, and Cagney's rather likable gangster hero was nicely offset by the despicable villains played by Humphrey Bogart

Humphrey Bogart and James Cagney

The story follows two boyhood friends, Rocky Sullivan (Cagney) and Jerry Connolly (Pat O'Brien), from their childhood on the "mean streets" of New York to their adult lives, when Rocky becomes a gangster and Jerry a priest. They are reunited when Rocky is released from a short prison term and decides to visit his old neighborhood, where Jerry is now the parish priest of the church where they had been altar boys together. Renting a room around the corner from the church, Rocky is also reunited with another childhood pal, Laury Martin (Sheridan), and befriends the Dead End Kids, a gang of slum boys who grow to worship him. Learning of the boys' affection for Sullivan, Father Jerry becomes concerned that Rocky might be a bad influence on them and inspire the kids to pursue a life of crime.

Meanwhile, Rocky visits his former henchman James Frazier (Bogart), who owes Rocky a large sum of money from a heist the two had pulled years earlier. Frazier and his new partner, racketeer Mac Keefer (Bancroft), promise both to pay Rocky his due and give him an interest in their lucrative nightspot, the El Toro. In reality, however, the two plan to murder Sullivan at the first opportunity, and they dispatch several torpedoes to do Rocky in. Later, Rocky and his would-be assassins have a bloody shoot-out at a local drugstore. Recognizing one of the killers as Frazier's bodyguard, Rocky realizes that Frazier and Keefer have double-crossed him. Appalled by the drugstore shooting, Father Jerry begins a fierce media campaign against crime, and, hearing of this, Frazier and Keefer make plans to murder him as well.

and George Bancroft, appearing as two rival gangleaders who attempt to double-cross Rocky. The love interest in the film was provided by another frequent co-star of Cagney's, Ann Sheridan, whose sensitive portrayal of the girl who loves Rocky provided *Angels With Dirty Faces* with many of its most touching moments. But aside from Cagney, the best performances in the picture were those delivered by Billy Halop, Leo Gorcey and the Dead End Kids, appearing as the neighborhood gang who come to idolize Cagney, much to the dismay of the priest played by O'Brien.

Once again, the New York East Side settings, designed by art director Robert Haas, greatly enhanced the proceedings, and particularly effective was the set representing the young gang's hideout, a dank basement fortress where the novice hoods plot their mischief. Also, *Angels With Dirty Faces* boasted an exceptionally well-made prologue, in which Rocky is shown as a boy being sent to reform school for petty theft. These scenes involving the youthful Rocky were superb, and their effect was enhanced by the fact that Frankie Burke, who played Sullivan in the prologue, bore an uncanny resemblance to Cagney and even sounded a great deal like him.

Bernard Punsley, Gabe Dell, Huntz Hall, Leo Gorcey, Bobby Jordan, Billy Halop and James Cagney

Seeing the opportunity to attain revenge and protect his boyhood chum at the same time, Rocky murders Frazier and Keefer in their offices at the nightclub. Minutes later, however, an army of police arrive at the scene and, completely out-gunned by the lawmen, Rocky is forced to surrender. Later, he is tried and convicted of murder, and sentenced to die in the electric chair. On the day of his execution, Rocky is visited by Jerry, who pleads with the condemned gangster to feign cowardice in the death chamber so that the Dead End Kids will "despise his memory." At first reluctant, Rocky breaks out in tearful pleas for his life at the last minute, and Father Jerry whispers a prayer for his salvation.

Angels With Dirty Faces was blessed with excellent photography by Sol Polito and a truly grand musical score by Max Steiner, both of which contributed to making the last scenes of the film among the most memorable of the genre. As Rocky is led by prison guards to the electric chair, Polito bathed the entire interlude in dark, oppressive shadows, and Steiner scored it with a plodding, relentless death march that beautifully captured the downbeat mood of Cagney's walk down the last mile.

Humphrey Bogart and James Cagney

James Cagney
and Pat O'Brien

58

THE AMAZING DR. CLITTERHOUSE

A WARNER BROTHERS PICTURE.   1938

Humphrey Bogart, Maxie Rosenbloom, Edward G. Robinson, Claire Trevor

CREDITS

Directed by Anatole Litvak. *Screenplay by* John Wexley and John Huston. *Based on the play by* Barre Lyndon. *Director of photography:* Tony Gaudio. *Film editor:* Warren Low. *Music by* Max Steiner. *Assistant director:* Jack Sullivan. *Art direction:* Carl Jules Weyl. *Dialogue director:* Jo Graham. *Wardrobe by* Milo Anderson. *Sound recording by* C.A. Riggs. *Running time:* 87 minutes.

CAST

Dr. Clitterhouse: Edward G. Robinson; *Jo:* Claire Trevor; *Rocks Valentine:* Humphrey Bogart; *Inspector Lane:* Donald Crisp; *Okay:* Allen Jenkins; *Nurse Randolph:* Gale Page; *Judge:* Henry O'Neill; *Prosecuter:* John Litel; *Grant:* Thurston Hall; *Butch:* Maxie Rosenbloom; *Rabbit:* Curt Bois; *Tug:* Ward Bond; *Pal:* Bert Hanlon; *Popus:* Vladimir Sokoloff.

Warner Brothers, ever in search of new and unusual story angles for their gangster films, really hit the jackpot with this one. The screenplay, by John Huston and John Wexley, was truly offbeat, telling the tale of a dedicated doctor who, for a time, becomes a gangster in order to carry

Claire Trevor and Humphrey Bogart

out first-hand research for a book he is writing on crime. The success of *Bullets or Ballots* and *Kid Galahad* prompted Warners to reteam Robinson and Bogart, with Robinson playing the doctor and Bogart appearing as the genuine gangster who serves as his guide to the underworld. The resulting film, blessed with a title that no one could forget, was called *The Amazing Dr. Clitterhouse* and it featured, in addition to the two gangster stars, a truly distinguished roster of character actors, including Donald Crisp (long a favorite on the Warners lot), Thurston Hall, John Litel, Henry O'Neill, Allan Jenkins and Maxie Rosenbloom.

Though admittedly just another standard crime melodrama, *The Amazing Dr. Clitterhouse* remains memorable for Robinson's excellent performance in the title role. Cast completely against type and obviously attempting to show the flipside of his tough-guy image, Robinson played the doctor as a gentle, cerebral milquetoast who, over the course of the story, gradually transforms into a criminal

Maxie Rosenbloom, Edward G. Robinson, Claire Trevor, Humphrey Bogart

mastermind as he commits crime after crime and slowly grows to enjoy it. Though much of the plot was rather far-fetched, audiences of the day remained fascinated by Robinson's character and the way in which the actor neatly handled Clitterhouse's clever transition from doctor to rackets boss.

The film contained excellent performances from Claire Trevor as the attractive fence who works with Robinson, and from Crisp, who had several fine scenes as a relentless police inspector. Bogart makes the most of his somewhat one-dimensional character, appearing in yet another of the surly hood roles he always played in films of this type. Bogart was still two years away from major stardom at the time of *The Amazing Dr. Clitterhouse* and it is safe to assume that the actor was growing weary of the monotonous parade of supporting heavies he seemed forever doomed to play.

As an interesting sidelight, Bogart would

Humphrey Bogart, Edward G. Robinson, Maxie Rosenbloom

Humphrey Bogart, Claire Trevor, Maxie Rosenbloom

frequently comment in later years that this film was one of his least favorites, as the character of Rocks Valentine, the shifty thug who teams up with Clitterhouse, gave him little chance to display his range and versatility. Though director Anatole Litvak revealed a definite talent for gangster pictures with his fine direction, *The Amazing Dr. Clitterhouse* turned out to be his first and only experience with the genre, and he spent the remainder of his career directing primarily romantic dramas, such as *All This and Heaven Too* (1940) and *Act of Love* (1953).

SYNOPSIS

Dr. Clitterhouse (Robinson), a respected member of the medical community, is writing a book on crime in modern society. Wanting to experience criminal actions first-hand, the doctor commits a series of successful jewel robberies, and sells the stuff through a gorgeous fence, Jo Keller (Claire Trevor). Meeting with her several times, Clitterhouse learns that Jo often acts as a fence for a gang of safecrackers headed by the notorious gangster, Rocks Valentine (Bogart). Clitterhouse subsequently becomes a temporary member of the gang, and during all of their succeeding robberies, the doctor carefully takes notes on the criminals' behavior patterns.

Meanwhile, Rocks becomes jealous when he learns that Jo is interested in the doctor romantically, and, during a warehouse robbery, Valentine locks Clitterhouse in a cold-storage vault, but he is luckily freed by Jo's good-hearted bodyguard, Butch (Maxie Rosenbloom). Leaving the gang to begin working on his book full time, the doctor is later accosted by Rocks, who threatens to expose the physician's criminal exploits unless Clitterhouse agrees to continue working with him. Realizing that the only crime he hasn't experienced first-hand is homicide, and that his book could benefit greatly from a chapter on the subject, Clitterhouse slips Rocks a poisoned drink. Later arrested for the murder of Valentine, the doctor goes on trial and, acting as his own lawyer, presents a brilliant, logical explanation for his actions, which the jury is unable to dispute, and he is acquitted.

Though *The Amazing Dr. Clitterhouse* was enjoyed by nearly everyone who saw it, many audience members had difficulty swallowing the ending, which, many thought, stretched the story's believability just a little *too* far.

Maxie Rosenbloom, Bert Hanlon, Allen Jenkins, Vladimir Sokoloff, Edward G. Robinson, Curt Bois, Ward Bond

RACKET BUSTERS

A WARNER BROTHERS PICTURE.   1938

Gloria Dickson and Humphrey Bogart

CREDITS

A Cosmopolitan Production. Directed by Lloyd Bacon. *Original screenplay by* Robert Rossen and Leonardo Bercovici. *Director of photography:* Arthur Edeson. *Associate producer:* Samuel Bischoff. *Film editor:* James Gibbon. *Music by* Adolph Deutsch. *Assistant director:* Dick Mayberry. *Art direction:* Esdras Hartley. *Gowns by* Howard Shoup. *Sound recording by* Robert B. Lee. *Running time:* 71 minutes.

CAST

Pete Martin: Humphrey Bogart; *Denny Jordan:* George Brent; *Nora Jordan:* Gloria Dickson; *Horse:* Allen Jenkins; *Thomas Allison:* Walter Abel; *Governor:* Henry O'Neill; *Gladys:* Penny Singleton; *Crane:* Anthony Averill; *Pop Wilson:* Oscar O'Shea; *Joe:* Joseph Downing; *Gus:* Norman Willis.

Though he was not awarded a starring role in a big-budget, first-class motion picture until *High Sierra*, released in 1940, Humphrey Bogart starred in several "second string" gangster pictures during the thirties, usually playing variations on the supporting heavies he portrayed in the Cagney–Robinson pictures. Though Bogart had little

respect for these medium-budget quickies, they provided the rising actor with a great deal of exposure and showed that he was definitely capable of carrying a film by himself. Though they lacked the big-budget polish of films like *Angels With Dirty Faces* and *The Roaring Twenties*, several of these minor Bogart pictures were quite good, and perhaps the best was *Racket Busters*, released in 1938.

Running a scant 71 minutes and obviously produced on a shoestring, *Racket Busters* is still extremely entertaining, managing to cram a great deal of action into its brief running time and provide its two stars, Humphrey Bogart and George Brent, with solid, three-dimensional roles. Bogart appeared as a gangster-tycoon named Pete Martin, who strongarms his way into control of the trucking business, and Brent played his adversary, a fiercely spirited truck driver who refuses to be intimidated by the racketeers. The scenes in

which Bogart and Brent confront each other were well acted, and Brent's fiery hero, Denny Jordan, genuinely touched audiences with his daring refusal to knuckle under to the corrupt gangster. Joseph Downing and Norman Willis were also most convincing as Bogart's murderous henchmen, and many scenes in the film were made more effective by their stony, malevolent faces leering in the background. There was also an excellent performance by Walter Abel as the special prosecutor hired by the D.A. to smash Bogart's crime syndicate, and Allen Jenkins, a frequent fixture in Warner Brothers gangster movies, also scored well as Brent's comic sidekick.

Though little more than a good guys versus the bad guys shoot-'em-up, *Racket Busters* was well directed by Lloyd Bacon, and became one of the most successful of the "B" gangster films starring Bogart.

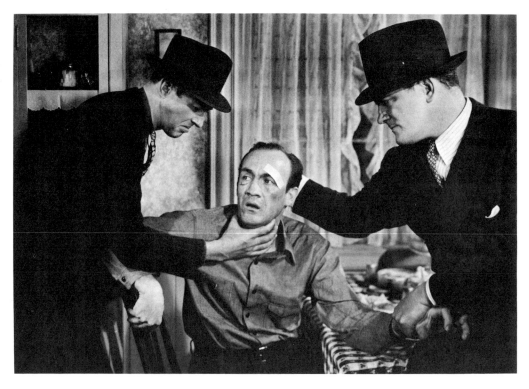

Norman Willis,
Elliott Sullivan, Don Rowan

Humphrey Bogart and George Brent

SYNOPSIS

The story takes place in New York City, where
Pete Martin (Bogart), a powerful crime czar, runs
a lucrative protection racket, in which small
businesses are forced to turn over half their
earnings to Martin's organization or suffer the
consequences. Seeking to expand his operation,
Martin wants to invade the trucking company that
supplies produce to the downtown markets.
Several truckers are attacked by Martin's henchmen while in route, and the terrified drivers gladly
begin shelling out their wages for protection. One
trucker who refuses to be intimidated, however, is
Denny Jordan (Brent), an honest, hard-working
man whose wife Nora (Gloria Dickson) is pregnant
with their first child.

Appalled that the rackets have invaded the
trucking industry, the District Attorney appoints a
brilliant lawyer, Thomas Allison (Walter Abel), as a
special prosecutor, whose job will be to gather
enough evidence on Martin and his gang to send
them to prison. When Allison questions the
truckers who were attacked, however, the frightened men refuse to tell him anything, which stalls

the prosecutor's efforts. Meanwhile, Martin learns of Jordan's refusal to knuckle under to extortion, and orders his accomplices to burn Denny's truck. Now without means of support and expecting his child any time, Jordan breaks into Martin's hideout and tries to steal some cash, but he is caught by the gangleader's men. Agreeing not to harm Denny if he starts paying off like the other truckers, Martin persuades the lone rebel to give in.

Now in complete control of the industry, Martin becomes worried when the local legislature passes a bill giving Allison the power to prosecute the truckers who refused to testify against the gangster. An older trucker named Pop Wilson (Oscar O'Shea) comes forward and presents Allison with evidence that incriminates Martin and his mob. Afterward, Wilson is brutally assassinated. An-

gered by the murder of their old friend, the truckers ban together and, with Allison's help, succeed in smashing the rackets.

Bogart's sneering portrayal of Pete Martin in *Racket Busters* was most effective, and the actor skillfully presented a portrait of a greedy, relentless mobster. He was matched every step of the way by George Brent's forceful playing as Denny Jordan and by Walter Abel's brisk, polished performance as the special prosecutor. The three actors obviously realized that *Racket Busters* was little more than a "B" programmer, but they also knew that they had a good script to work with. Because of this, they gave the minor vehicle everything they had, and the results were rewarding.

Gloria Dickson and George Brent

67

KING OF THE UNDERWORLD

A WARNER BROTHERS PICTURE.   1939

Humphrey Bogart, Kay Francis, James Stephenson

CREDITS

Directed by Lewis Seiler. *Screenplay by* George Bricker and Vincent Sherman. *Director of photography:* Sid Hickox. *Film editor:* Frank Dewar. *Music by* Heinz Roemheld. *Dialogue director:* Vincent Sherman. *Assistant director:* Frank Heath. *Art direction:* Charles Novi. *Gowns by* Orry-Kelly. *Sound recording by* Everett A. Brown. *Running time:* 69 minutes.

CAST

Joe Gurney: Humphrey Bogart; *Carol Nelson:* Kay Francis; *Bill Forrest:* James Stephenson; *Niles:* John Eldredge; *Aunt Margaret:* Jessie Busley; *Sheriff:* Raymond Brown; *Eddie:* Charley Foy; *Porky:* Joe Devlin; *Slick:* Alan Davis; *Slats:* John Harmon; *Jerry:* John Ridgely; *Interne:* Richard Bond.

King of the Underworld was produced right on the heels of *Racket Busters* and was, once again, a low-budget gangster melodrama showcasing the talents of Humphrey Bogart. What makes this picture perhaps more interesting to film students than Bogart's other gangster quickies is that it gave him a good, solid character to play, one with considerably more dimension and depth than the other bad guys he was playing during this period. The part of Joe Gurney, a rackets boss with delusions of grandeur and a monumental ego, gave Bogart the chance to tackle a truly complex and challenging role for a change, and the actor's forceful portrayal of the vicious gangster was his finest screen work since *The Petrified Forest* and *Dead End*. This was no run-of-the-mill thug, but a twisted, psychopathic personality, who takes sadistic delight in dominating those around him and who views himself as a kind of Napoleon of crime, a man who dreams of one day becoming the center of all criminal activity, a true king of the underworld.

The picture's quality was also enhanced by the fact that Warners gave Bogart the elegant Kay Francis for a co-star, and her presence in the picture lent it a distinct aura of class, and lifted it above most other grade "B" shoot-em-ups. Her role, that of a female doctor who becomes an unwilling accomplice to Bogart and his gang, was also three-dimensional and believable, and Francis

Humphrey Bogart, Kay Francis, James Stephenson

Humphrey Bogart and Kay Francis

69

presented a convincing portrait of an intelligent, strong-willed woman trapped by circumstances into aiding criminals. The script by George Bricker (one of Hollywood's all-time great writers of "B" material) and Vincent Sherman (who was only a few years away from emerging as a top-flight director at Warners) also contained secondary characters who were much more finely drawn than usual. A good example of this is the brilliant young writer (played by rising Warner contract player James Stephenson) who also unwittingly becomes involved with Bogart and who is forced, under threat of death, to write the egomanical gangster's life story. Stephenson, a tall, handsome Englishman, with a gentlemanly, distinguished aura about him, also helped give *King of the Underworld* a somewhat classier feel than *Racket Busters, Dr. Clitterhouse* and the like, and he portrayed the young author as a fiercely ambitious artist, fascinated by the opportunity to write the gangster's biography while at the same time realizing the danger involved. Stephenson's fine work in this low-budget crime drama was, in many ways, a prelude to his best-known performance as the lawyer in Bette Davis's 1940 classic *The Letter*.

SYNOPSIS

The story begins as a husband and wife doctor team, Niles and Carol Nelson (John Eldredge and Kay Francis), save the life of a wounded man, unaware that he is a henchman of gangleader Joe Gurney (Bogart). When Gurney eventually meets the couple, he devises a scheme to gain control over their lives. Learning that Niles has a weakness for gambling, Gurney begins loaning him large sums of money, which are promptly lost at the bookmakers. Gurney agrees to forget about the money if the doctor promises to come to the gang's aid whenever any of them need medical attention. Later, another of Gurney's men is shot, and Niles is forced to treat him. When Gurney's hideout is raided by police sometime afterward, he suspects the doctor of squealing, and he murders him. Learning of Niles's involvement with Gurney, the authorities begin suspecting that he and Carol were willing accomplices to the criminals.

To escape prosecution for crimes that she did not commit, Carol moves to a small town where, coincidentally, two of Gurney's men are being held in the local jail. Meanwhile, Gurney, who fancies himself something of a celebrity, kidnaps Bill Forrest (Stephenson), a young writer hitch-hiking across the country. The gangster orders Forrest to begin writing Gurney's biography, which will be titled *King of the Underworld*. Arriving in the small town where his two men are jailed, Gurney frees them, but is wounded during a skirmish with police. Learning that Carol has set up a small practice in town, Gurney goes to see her, seeking medical aid. Pretending that she now wants to become his accomplice for real, Carol sets Gurney up for the cops in an effort to clear herself. She deliberately infects Gurney's gunshot wound, and then blinds the gangster and his men with eyedrops she pretends will halt the spread of infection. The police then close in, and Gurney is shot to death.

King of the Underworld was directed by Lewis Seiler, who had directed Bogart in an earlier Warner film called *Crime School* (1938), and who would later guide the actor through yet another gangster opus, *The Big Shot* (1942).

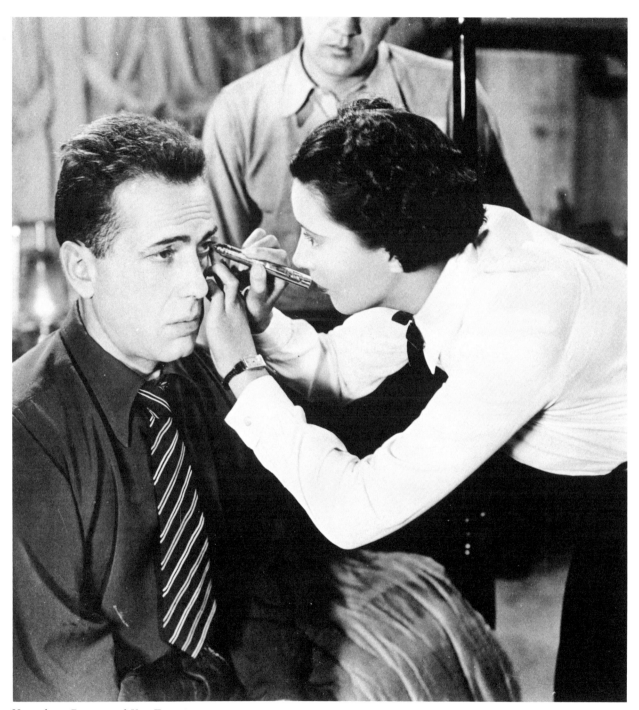

Humphrey Bogart and Kay Francis

THE ROARING TWENTIES

A WARNER BROTHERS PICTURE.   1939

Frank McHugh, Jeffrey Lynn, Gladys George, James Cagney, Priscilla Lane, Humphrey Bogart, Paul Kelly

Frank McHugh, James Cagney, Humphrey Bogart

Frank McHugh and James Cagney

CREDITS

Directed by Raoul Walsh. *Executive producer:* Hal B. Wallis. *Associate producer:* Samuel Bischoff. *Screenplay by* Jerry Wald, Richard Macaulay and Robert Rossen. *Based on an original story by* Mark Hellinger. *Director of photography:* Ernest Haller. *Music by* Heinz Roemheld and Ray Heindorf. *Film editor:* Jack Killifer. *Dialogue director:* Hugh Cummings. *Assistant director:* Dick Mayberry. *Art direction:* Max Parker. *Sound recording by* Everett A. Brown. *Running time:* 106 minutes.

CAST

Eddie Bartlett: James Cagney; *Jean Sherman:* Priscilla Lane; *George Hally:* Humphrey Bogart; *Panama Smith:* Gladys George; *Lloyd Hart:* Jeffrey Lynn; *Danny Green:* Frank McHugh; *Nick Brown:* Paul Kelly; *Mrs. Sherman:* Elisabeth Risdon; *Sgt. Jones:* Joseph Sawyer; *Henderson:* Edward Keane; *Masters:* George Meeker; *Judge:* John Hamilton.

Mark Hellinger's colorful, dramatic chronicle of the prohibition era—*The Roaring Twenties*—was one of the most popular and widely read stories of its day, and in 1940 it was brought to the screen in the form of a lavish, handsomely dressed Warner Brothers gangster vehicle starring James Cagney. Three top writers—Jerry Wald, Richard McCauley and Robert Rossen—worked on the screenplay for the film, and Cagney was given his usual splendid supporting cast, including Priscilla Lane, Humphrey Bogart, Jeffrey Lynn, Gladys George, Frank McHugh, Paul Kelly and Joseph Sawyer, and one of Warners' front-ranking directors, Raoul Walsh. In tackling his first gangster picture, Walsh approached the material in a somewhat lighter vein than did William Wellman and Michael Curtiz in *The Public Enemy* and *Angels With Dirty Faces*, shading *The Roaring Twenties* with more comic relief than usual and downplaying the scenes of gangland violence.

The director also injected *The Roaring Twenties* with a far more romantic mood than was seen in previous gangster pictures, and Cagney's tender crush on Priscilla Lane gave his character, Eddie Bartlett, a softness and vulnerability that the earlier Tom Powers and Rocky Sullivan were lacking. And although he wasn't nominated for Best Actor in the 1940 Oscar race, Cagney's portrayal of Bartlett, the small-time hood who rises

James Cagney *(c)*

Humphrey Bogart and James Cagney

to the top as a bootlegger only to plummet into poverty and alcoholism, was certainly equal to his Oscar-nominated work in *Angels,* especially in the scenes toward the end of the film, when Eddie becomes a pathetic shadow of his former self. Sitting in a chintzy bar, his mind clouded with whiskey and endlessly reminiscing about the good old days, Cagney beautifully captured the mood and mannerisms of a melancholy drunkard, and his subtle playing of a boozy down-and-outer was

The story begins as Eddie Bartlett (Cagney) returns home to New York after heroic service in World War I. Though highly decorated for bravery overseas, Eddie finds that his medals mean very little in the civilian world and, after weeks of pounding the pavement, he is unable to secure even menial employment. Desperate, he moves in with his old friend Danny Green (Frank McHugh) and the two begin operating a taxi service. While on the job one afternoon, Eddie enters a speakeasy by mistake, and is introduced to the bootlegging business by the club's owner, Panama Smith (Gladys George). Abandoning his cab driving job, Eddie begins manufacturing illegal whiskey in his apartment, and soon he and Danny become full-time racketeers.

nothing short of brilliant. As in *Angels With Dirty Faces,* Bogart was cast as Cagney's gangland rival, and the picture was to have originally featured Ann Sheridan as Panama Smith, the lady speakeasy owner who falls in love with Cagney. Before filming got underway, however, the studio decided that the lovely Sheridan was completely unsuited to the rather hard-edged character and she was replaced by Gladys George, who gave a memorable performance.

Priscilla Lane and James Cagney

Later, Eddie learns that his old buddy from the army, George Hally (Humphrey Bogart) is also in the rum-running business, and is his only serious competition. When Eddie suggests to George that they join forces, George agrees, and he and Eddie attain great wealth by forming the biggest bootlegging operation in New York. The partnership goes smoothly for awhile, but soon Eddie grows disenchanted with Hally's strongarm tactics, and the two end their association. When prohibition is repealed, Eddie's fortunes dwindle and he takes to the bottle to ease the loss. Becoming an alcoholic, Eddie sinks lower and lower into drunken despair, while George grows richer by entering other fields of criminal activity. When George's gang kills Danny in a shoot-out, Eddie goes to Hally's apartment and slays his former partner. Running from the building, Eddie is shot in the back by one of George's henchmen, and dies on the steps of a nearby church.

The Roaring Twenties was perhaps the most lavishly produced of all the classic Warner Brothers gangster films, and it remains a top-flight entertainment.

Humphrey Bogart, Al Hill and James Cagney

YOU CAN'T GET AWAY WITH MURDER

A WARNER BROTHERS PICTURE.   1939

Billy Halop, Humphrey Bogart, Harold Huber

CREDITS

Directed by Lewis Seiler. *Screenplay by* Robert Buckner, Don Ryan and Kenneth Gamet. *Associate producer:* Samuel Bischoff. *Director of photography:* Sol Polito. *Music by* Heinz Roemheld. *Film editor:* James Gibbon. *Dialogue director:* Jo Graham. *Art direction:* Hugh Reticker. *Assistant director:* William Kissel. *Gowns by* Milo Anderson. *Sound recording by* Francis J. Scheid. *Running time:* 78 minutes.

CAST

Frank Wilson: Humphrey Bogart; *Johnnie Stone:* Billy Halop; *Madge:* Gale Page; *Fred Burke:* Harvey Stephens; *Scappa:* Harold Huber; *Carey:* John Litel; *Pop:* Henry Travers; *Red:* Joseph Sawyer; *Smitty:* Joseph Downing; *Toad:* George E. Stone.

Though little more than a low-budget programmer, *You Can't Get Away With Murder* was a fast-moving and thoroughly enjoyable crime drama, featuring Humphrey Bogart and Billy Halop in the leading roles. With his seemingly endless string of grade "B" gangster pictures, Bogart was fast gaining a reputation as one of the screen's favorite badmen, and Halop was well known to audiences

Joe Downing, Harold Huber, Humphrey Bogart

as the leader of the popular Dead End Kids. Since both projected a similar quality on screen—a tough, cynical exterior masking a kind and soft-hearted nature—it seemed a natural to team the actors in a vehicle specially built around their talents.

To Warners' delight, the combination of Bogart and Halop clicked with the movie-going public, and *You Can't Get Away With Murder* became a formidable box office success.

There was, of course, little that was new or original in the script by Robert Buckner, Don Ryan and Kenneth Gamet, and it simply presented Bogart and Halop with roles obviously modelled after the characters they had played in the original *Dead End*. Bogart appeared as yet another villainous racketeer whose early life forced him into crime, and Halop again played the impressionable slum kid who falls in with the big-time criminal. Audiences were more than willing to overlook the fact that they had, in a sense, seen it all before, and clearly enjoyed all the action and melodrama.

Briskly directed by Lewis Seiler, *You Can't Get Away With Murder* featured, in addition to Bogart and Halop, a supporting cast that was rife with members of the Warner Brothers gangster movie stock company, including such familiar faces as Henry Travers, Joseph Sawyer, John Ridgely, George E. Stone and Harold Huber. Though their roles amounted to little more than cameos, these venerable character actors contributed enormously to the picture's atmosphere and mood.

SYNOPSIS

Reared in the slums and seeing little chance for escape, young Johnnie Stone (Halop) turns to crime as a way out of his environment, and he

Humphrey Bogart, Billy Halop, Joe Downing

Harvey Stevens, Joseph King, Joseph Crehan

forms an alliance with a veteran criminal named Fred Wilson (Bogart). Their first job—the robbery of an all-night gas station—goes off like a charm, and Johnnie becomes intoxicated by the thrill of breaking the law. Completely under the gangster's spell, Johnnie obeys Wilson's order to steal a gun, and he takes the one owned by his sister Madge's fiancé, Fred Burke (Harvey Stephens). Wilson and Johnnie use the gun in the robbery of a pawnshop, but this time things do not go smoothly and Wilson is forced to kill the pawnbroker. Later, the

police trace the murder weapon to Burke, who is arrested for the crime and subsequently sentenced to die in the electric chair at Sing Sing.

Seeing that Burke's imprisonment is causing Madge great unhappiness, Johnnie's conscience begins to gnaw at him, but Wilson's vicious death threats keep the boy from clearing Burke. Meanwhile, Johnnie and Wilson are arrested during an attempted auto theft, and are both given stretches in Sing Sing as well. The harsh brutality of prison life begins to wear Johnnie down and, realizing that Burke's impending execution will destroy his sister, he is overcome by the urge to tell what he knows regardless of consequences. Wilson, however, orders the boy to accompany him on a daring escape attempt, during which the prison guards manage to trap the two escapees in a railroad boxcar. Wilson shoots Johnnie, who confesses the truth to the cops before dying. This clears Burke, and Wilson is condemned to take his place on death row.

Though hardly in the same league with films like *The Public Enemy* and *Angels With Dirty Faces,* the compelling chemistry generated by Bogart and Halop in their familiar tough guy roles more than compensated for *You Can't Get Away With Murder*'s rather economical production values.

Billy Halop and
Humphrey Bogart

80

BROTHER ORCHID

A WARNER BROTHERS PICTURE.   1940

Edward G. Robinson (1)

CREDITS

Directed by Lloyd Bacon. *Executive producer:* Hal B. Wallis. *Associate producer:* Mark Hellinger. *Screenplay by* Earl Baldwin. *Director of photography:* Tony Gaudio. *Film editor:* William Holmes. *Music by* Heinz Roemheld. *Dialogue director:* Hugh Cummings. *Assistant director:* Dick Mayberry. *Art direction:* Max Parker. *Gowns by* Howard Shoup. *Make-up by* Perc Westmore. *Sound recording by* C. A. Riggs. *Running time:* 91 minutes.

CAST

Little John Sarto: Edward G. Robinson; *Flo Addams:* Ann Sothern; *Jack Buck:* Humphrey Bogart; *Brother Superior:* Donald Crisp; *Clarence Fletcher:* Ralph Bellamy; *Willie the Knife:* Allen Jenkins; *Brother Goodwin:* Cecil Kellaway; *Curley Matthews:* Tom Tyler.

Brother Orchid, the last of the Robinson–Bogart pictures (discounting *Key Largo*, which was not really part of the original Warners gangster cycle), was also one of the last great gangster comedies. Rumor has it that Robinson, having grown tired of gangster parts after playing them for nearly ten years, originally refused to appear in *Brother Orchid*, and agreed to make the picture only after Warners promised to give him the lead in the

John Ridgely (*1*) and Ralph Bellamy (*c*)

upcoming production of Jack London's *The Sea Wolf*. If this story is true, then it serves to illustrate the point that Robinson, Bogart and Cagney were, whether they liked it or not, type cast in the gangster mold to a certain degree, despite the fact that each had impressive credits away from the genre. This was especially true in Robinson's case as, throughout the thirties, he had appeared in more crime dramas than any other actor, and every one of them had been a solid box office hit.

The studio was well aware that the film-going public relished seeing the popular Robinson in gangster roles and, according to gossip, pressured the star to take the lead in *Brother Orchid* by threatening to give the juicy role of Wolf Larson to someone else. Film fans can indeed be thankful that Robinson decided to go along with the studio's terms, for his performance in *The Sea Wolf*, released later in the year, was nothing short of magnificent, and *Brother Orchid* turned out to be a thoroughly charming satire on the whole gangster genre. Perhaps realizing that *Brother Orchid* might well be Robinson's last gangster picture, Warners gave it a vigorous publicity campaign

Ann Sothern and Edward G. Robinson

upon its release, and designed one of the most colorful and innovative display posters ever afforded one of their gangster epics. It featured an outsized caricature of the actor, cigar in mouth, decked out in fancy evening dress, including a top hat and spats, giving a sly wink and pointing to his name, which appeared above the title in huge, cartoon-like letters. This unique poster gave most who saw it the hint that *Brother Orchid* was in no way a serious shoot-'em-up like *Little Caesar* and was more of a tongue-in-cheek spoof. As had been the case in all their pictures together, Robinson and Bogart played deadly adversaries who eventually come to blows. This time, however, it was decided that, because of the light-hearted tone of the story, another pistol duel might be inappropriate, so a rousing fist-fight was staged instead, during which the two stars beat each other to a pulp.

SYNOPSIS

Returning from a holiday in Europe, rackets boss Little John Sarto (Robinson) finds that, while

Ralph Bellamy and Ann Sothern

Paul Phillips, Morgan Conway, Humphrey Bogart, Edward G. Robinson

83

Edward G. Robinson and Allen Jenkins

Edward G. Robinson, Ann Sothern, Ralph Bellamy

he was away, his gang was taken over by his arch rival, Jack Buck (Bogart). Refusing Buck's offer to become second-in-command, Sarto forms a new organization of his own, and begins a running war with Buck and his mob. Trying to fix it so that Little John will stay out of the way permanently, Buck's men take him for a ride, but the quick-thinking Sarto manages to escape his abductors. Wounded while fleeing, however, Sarto makes his way to a monastery in the country, where he is nursed back to health by the monks who live there. When he recovers, Sarto is shown around the quiet retreat by the beneficent Brother Superior (Donald Crisp), who invites the mobster to stay as long as he likes. He is told by the Brother that even temporary residents like himself must "toil for the benefit of the Brotherhood," and, thinking the place an ideal hideout, Sarto decides to play along, taking a job tending the monastery's beautiful flower garden.

Christened Brother Orchid by the monks, Sarto begins to admire these selfless, devoted men who live such a clean and wholesome life. Soon, he becomes a master flower grower, selling his prize creations to flower shops in town and turning over the proceeds to Brother Superior. Later, Sarto learns that Buck, having heard of Little John's work at the monastery, has threatened great harm to any dealers purchasing his flowers. Returning to the city, Sarto confronts Buck, and the two become embroiled in a brutal fist-fight, during which Buck is beaten into submission. After smashing Buck's gang, Sarto returns to the monastery, and tells Brother Superior that he has decided to stay on forever.

One of the all-time favorites of the Warners gangster cycle, *Brother Orchid* was a thoroughly delightful diversion, and the studio managed to somehow persuade Robinson to appear in another gangland comedy the following year, *Larceny, Inc.*

IT ALL CAME TRUE

A WARNER BROTHERS PICTURE.   1940

Ann Sheridan and Humphrey Bogart

CREDITS

Directed by Lewis Seiler. *Executive producer:* Hal B. Wallis. *Associate producer:* Mark Hellinger. *Screenplay by* Michael Fessier and Lawrence Kimble. *Director of photography:* Ernest Haller. *Music by* Heinz Roemheld. *Film editor:* Thomas Richards. *Dialogue director:* Robert Foulk. *Assistant director:* Russ Saunders. *Art direction:* Max Parker. *Gowns by* Howard Shoup. *Make-up by* Perc Westmore. *Sound recording by* Dolph Thomas. *Running Time:* 97 minutes.

Jeffrey Lynn and Ann Sheridan

CAST

Sarah Jane Ryan: Ann Sheridan; *Tommy Taylor:* Jeffrey Lynn; *Chips Maguire:* Humphrey Bogart; *Maggie Ryan:* Una O'Connor; *Norah Taylor:* Jessie Busley; *Mr. Roberts:* John Litel; *Mr. Salmon:* Grant Mitchell; *Mr. Boldini:* Felix Bressart.

It All Came True, an interesting attempt by Warners to incorporate comedy and music into a

gangster picture, represented one of Bogart's last supporting performances, and was released only months before the actor achieved stardom in *High Sierra.* Despite the fact that he was given third billing behind Ann Sheridan and Jeffrey Lynn, Bogart turned out to be the main attraction in this modest but entertaining film, and this time, surprisingly enough, his tough, cynical gangster was allowed to redeem himself and actually become the hero of the piece. This proved especially enjoyable to audiences, and no doubt to Bogart as well, who, for once, was playing something more than just a despicable villain who gets his in the final reel.

Though roles of this kind had kept him one of the busiest and best paid supporting actors of the thirties, Bogart deeply resented being type cast as a heel, and must have certainly regarded *It All Came True,* in which his bad guy turns out to have a heart of gold, as an all-too-welcome change of pace. The script also fashioned for Bogart several interludes in which, rather uncharacteristically, he was required to indulge in some broad comedy—the scenes in which his harried gangster reluctantly finds himself in the care of two old biddies, played by Una O'Connor and Jessie Busley, who wait on him hand and foot. Playing against these two veteran actresses, whose comic timing and delivery were impeccable, Bogart surprised everybody by displaying an unsuspected flair for comedy. His somewhat tongue-in-cheek portrayal of a gangster in *It All Came True* is one of the best and most overlooked performances of the actor's pre-stardom era, and he stole the picture completely from Sheridan and Lynn, who appeared in rather dry, conventional romantic leads.

Interestingly, *It All Came True* was quite unlike the very "cinematic" Warner gangster movies of a few years earlier, and had a distinctly stage-like feel to it, almost as if the material had been based on a play (which it was not). This was perhaps due to the fact that, for the most part, the story revolved around a single setting—the rundown boarding house where Bogart's gangster takes refuge. The picture also differed from its predecessors in that there was little violence or gunplay, with the exception of the early scene in which Bogart guns down a police officer. Bogart, at the very brink of the stardom that had eluded him so long, was especially well served by the Warner

Brothers costume department, and he appeared in a variety of truly stylish and dapper outfits, which added enormously to the appeal of his character.

SYNOPSIS

The story takes place in a theatrical boarding house run by Maggie Ryan (Una O'Connor) and Nora Taylor (Jessie Busley). Their grown children, Sarah Jane (Sheridan) and Tommy (Lynn), live there as well, and are both struggling show business hopefuls. When Chips Maguire (Bogart), an imfamous gangster, kills a policeman with Tommy's gun, Tommy, in order to protect himself from being blamed for the crime, offers the killer refuge at the boarding house. In an effort to keep the criminal's identity a secret, Tommy introduces Maguire as Mr. Grasselli, a friend recently recovered from a nervous breakdown who will need continual bedrest. However, Sarah, who once worked as a torch singer in a nightclub owned by Maguire, recognizes him.

Meanwhile, Maguire is tended by Maggie and Nora, who nearly drive the gangster crazy with their motherly concern. In order to escape their attentions, Maguire goes downstairs to the sitting room, where he is treated to a "variety show" put on by Sarah, Tommy and some of the other tenants. Impressed by their talents, Maguire offers the financial backing necessary to convert the place into a nightclub. Over the succeeding weeks, the rundown boarding house is magically transformed into a posh nightspot, where Tommy and Sarah will be the featured attraction. On opening night, however, the police show up with a warrant for Tommy's arrest, having traced the young man's gun. At the last minute, however, Maguire goes sentimental and admits to the killing, thereby clearing Tommy.

It All Came True, despite the overt schmaltz and corn, scored well at the box office. In addition to the fine role it gave Bogart, the picture also provided Ann Sheridan the opportunity to display her singing talents in two nicely staged numbers, "Angel in Disguise" and "The Way of the Gaucho."

Ann Sheridan and Humphrey Bogart

CASTLE ON THE HUDSON

A WARNER BROTHERS PICTURE.   1940

John Garfield

John Garfield

Publicity shot with director
Anatole Litvak and John Garfield

CREDITS

Directed by Anatole Litvak. *Screenplay by* Seton I. Miller, Brown Holmes and Courtney Terrett. *From the book by* warden Lewis E. Lawes. *Director of photography:* Arthur Edeson. *Art direction:* John Hughes. *Dialogue director:* Irving Rapper. *Film editor:* Thomas Richards. *Sound by* Robert B. Lee. *Music by* Adolph Deutsch. *Musical director:* Leo F. Forbstein. *Gowns by* Howard Shoup. *Make-up by* Perc Westmore. *Special effects by* Byron Haskin and Edwin DuPar. *Running time:* 77 minutes.

CAST

Tommy Gordon: John Garfield; *Kay:* Ann Sheri-dan; *Warden Long:* Pat O'Brien; *Steven Rockford:* Burgess Meredith; *Ed Crowley:* Jerome Cowan; *District Attorney:* Henry O'Neill; *Mike Kagel:* Guinn Williams; *Prison Chaplain:* John Litel; *Black Jack:* Edward Pawley; *Dr. Ames:* Grant Mitchell; *Ann:* Margot Stevenson; *Ragan:* Willard Robertson; *Clyde Burton:* Robert Homans; *Mrs. Long:* Nedda Harrigan; *Principal Keeper:* Wade Boteler; *Pete:* Billy Wayne; *Gangster:* Joseph Downing; *Blonde:* Barbara Pepper; *Morris:* Robert Strange.

The success of the Robinson–Cagney–Bogart pictures prompted Warners to fashion several gangster vehicles for another of its popular stars,

Every Scene Crackles with GARFIELD Excitement!

JOHN
GARFIELD
ANN
SHERIDAN
PAT
O'BRIEN

CASTLE
ON THE
HUDSON

A WARNER BROS. RE-RELEASE

BURGESS MEREDITH AN ANATOLE LITVAK
PRODUCTION
Screen Play by Seton I. Miller, Brown Holmes and
Courtney Terrett • From the Book by Lewis E. Lawes
A Warner Bros.-First National Picture

ties as a gangster prior to his arrest, no doubt because Warners, determined to make Garfield a gangster star, made *Castle on the Hudson* more of a *gangster* film than the original.

Though the picture holds up well today, with Garfield, Ann Sheridan and Pat O'Brien delivering fine performances, *Castle on the Hudson,* at the time of its release, did not fare especially well with critics, many of whom remarked that Garfield seemed ill-suited to the gangster cinema and should return to straight dramas. Interestingly, Garfield actually objected to the studio's trying to make him into another Cagney, and tried to pursuade Warners to refrain from casting him in gangster pictures, a genre he apparently had little affection for.

In spite of everything, however, *Castle on the Hudson* remains an entertaining, well-mounted crime picture, containing some truly atmospheric prison scenes, not unlike the 1932 version. And Garfield, despite what the critics of the day said, made a splendid gangster, imbuing his character with a dash of sexy arrogance not unlike that of Cagney's classic Tom Powers. He also looked the part to a "T", and in his suave black fedora and stylish tuxedo might easily have passed for a genuine racketeer. Ann Sheridan provided Garfield with excellent support as the good-hearted girl whom he loves (the role originated by Bette Davis in the earlier version). The vibrant black-and-white photography of Arthur Edeson gave *Castle on the Hudson* a look and feel similar to *Angels With Dirty Faces,* as did the presence of Pat O'Brien, appearing as the compassionate warden of the prison. Burgess Meredith had a juicy supporting role as one of the convicts Garfield meets during his stay in the big house, and Jerome Cowan also scored well as a shifty, double-dealing lawyer.

SYNOPSIS

Tommy Gordon (Garfield), a slick young gangster, is arrested and sent to Sing Sing prison, also known as the "Castle on the Hudson." Warden Lord (Pat O'Brien), a strong advocate of convict rehabilitation, takes a personal interest in Tommy

John Garfield. The studio felt that the actor's tough, rebellious screen image would make him a natural for crime films, and in the early forties they produced a string of well-made gangster pictures starring Garfield.

The movies were *Castle on the Hudson* (1940), *East of the River* (1940) and *Out of the Fog* (1941) and, of the three, *Castle on the Hudson* perhaps came closest to recapturing some of the glory of the earlier Warners classics. The film was a virtual remake of the famous prison drama *20,000 Years in Sing Sing* (1932), with Garfield assuming the role originated by Spencer Tracy. The remake differed from the original, however, in that there was far more footage devoted to Garfield's activi-

Ann Sheridan, Jerome Cowan, John Garfield

upon discovering that his intelligence is far above
that of the average prisoner. Soon, the warden
befriends the young racketeer and tries to dis-
suade him from returning to crime once he's
released. Meanwhile, one of Tommy's fellow
inmates (Burgess Meredith) is secretly engineering a prison break, but Tommy refuses to partici-
pate because it will take place on a Saturday,
Tommy's "unlucky day."

In town, Tommy's crooked attorney (Jerome
Cowan) seeks to seize all of the young gangster's
fortune, and he even makes advances toward
Tommy's girlfriend Kay (Sheridan). Later, Kay is
seriously injured in an auto accident and sent to
the hospital to recover. Wanting to see her, Tommy
secures the warden's permission to visit Kay upon
the stipulation that he return to Sing Sing within
forty-eight hours. When Kay tells Tommy about
the lawyer's treachery, however, the gangster

Burgess Meredith and John Garfield

remains in town, breaking his promise to the warden. Tommy stays on the outside for the next few weeks, and plots a deadly revenge on his scheming attorney. Released from the hospital, Kay recuperates in a small hotel room, where she is visited by the lawyer, who tries to take advantage of her once again. Suddenly, however, Tommy arrives and, when the two men get into a fight, Kay kills the lawyer. In order to save Kay from a murder charge, Tommy returns to Sing Sing and takes the rap himself.

Several months after *Castle on the Hudson's* release, Garfield made another gangster picture for Warners called *East of the River,* which proved to be nothing more than a routine shoot-'em-up, totally lacking the entertainment value of its predecessor.

John Garfield and Burgess Meredith

BLACK FRIDAY

A UNIVERSAL PICTURE.   1940

Boris Karloff

CREDITS

Directed by Arthur Lubin. *Produced by* Burt Kelly. *Screenplay by* Curt Siodmak and Erick Taylor. *Director of photography:* Elwood Bredell. *Art direction:* Jack Otterson. *Set decoration:* Russell A. Gausman. *Music by* Hans J. Salter and Frank Skinner. *Special effects by* John P. Fulton. *Costumes by* Vera West. *Make-up by* Jack P. Pierce. *Running time:* 69 minutes.

CAST

Dr. Ernest Sovac: Boris Karloff; *Eric Marnay/ Professor Kingsley:* Bela Lugosi; *Red Cannon:*

Boris Karloff

Boris Karloff

Stanley Ridges; *Sunny Rogers:* Anne Nagel; *Jean Sovac:* Anne Gwynne; *Margaret:* Virginia Brissac; *Frank Miller:* Edmund MacDonald; *Kane:* Paul Fix; *Bellhop:* Murray Alper; *Bartender:* Jack Mulhall; *Police Chief:* Joe King; *Taxi Driver:* John Kelly.

The prize for a unique gangster movie concept must go to Universal Pictures, who, in 1940, conceived of combining that popular genre with the one that they had become specialists in—the horror film. The studio was, at that time, just beginning its second horror film cycle, and had been quite pleased by the success of the previous year's blockbuster, *Son of Frankenstein.* The gangster-horror film project began shooting in early 1940 under the working title *Friday the 13th,* and its box office success was practically assured by the fact that the studio persuaded its two biggest thriller stars, Boris Karloff and Bela Lugosi, to appear as a screen team once again.

The plot of *Friday the 13th* concerned a brilliant doctor who transplants the brain of a gangster into the skull of a dying professor friend in order to save his life. Of course, complications arise as the genial professor soon finds himself periodically transforming into the gangster and killing off the dead man's enemies. The concept was obviously a combination of story elements from Karloff's own *Frankenstein* and another popular and oft-filmed horror tale, *Dr. Jekyll and Mr. Hyde.* Originally, Karloff and Lugosi had roles of equal stature in the film, with Lugosi playing the doctor and Karloff the mild-mannered professor. Shortly after the filming began, however, the studio discovered that the suave, elegant Karloff seemed completely miscast during those scenes that required him to change into the crude, laconic gangster, Red Cannon. The studio hired a more suitable actor, Stanley Ridges, to play the Jekyll-Hyde professor, and gave the part of the brain surgeon to Karloff. Poor Lugosi found himself reduced to a thankless supporting role as the big shot gangster who double-crosses Cannon and is done in for his treachery.

Anne Nagel, Stanley Ridges, Bela Lugosi

The film was released in March of 1940 with a slightly more commercial title, *Black Friday*, with Karloff and Lugosi sharing equal billing despite the fact that the latter's part amounted to little more than a cameo. This little mish-mash of the gangster and horror genres remains one of the most overlooked of Universal's vintage shockers. Though it contained all the earmarks of the studio's horror series (like the familiar H. J. Salter-Frank Skinner "monster themes" as background music, shadowy close-ups of Karloff giving his well-known hypnotic stare, and the flavorful settings and photography), *Black Friday* was unfortunately marred to some degree by its less than convincing gangster scenes. The shootouts in the picture were laughably bad, and the characters of Lugosi and his henchmen were little more than stereotypes. As a gangster picture, *Black Friday* didn't even come close to the high water mark established by Warners, but the horrific elements in the film were something else again, and their effect was enhanced by the use of snatches from the superb *Son of Frankenstein* musical score

(such as the wonderful violin "laboratory" leitmotif, used here to underscore the scenes of Karloff preparing for the brain transplantation). Stanley Ridges handled his two-part role with skill, somewhat overshadowing the two horror stars and creating a truly memorable character.

SYNOPSIS

When Dr. Sovac (Karloff) and his friend Professor Kingsley (Ridges) stumble into a gangland shootout by accident, Kingsley is seriously injured. He is rushed to the hospital along with Red Cannon, one of the gangsters who was hurt in the exchange. Realizing that Kingsley will die from his massive injuries, Sovac saves his life by transplanting Cannon's brain into Kingsley's skull. When Kingsley is taken home to recover sometime later, Sovac observes that the professor's consciousness is being taken over from time to time by the criminal's. Learning that the gangster has $500,000 in stolen loot hidden somewhere in New York City, Sovac suggests to Kingsley that they

95

holiday there, and, once they arrive, the doctor takes Kingsley to several of Red Cannon's old haunts. The gangster's memories begin to surface with greater regularity and, not long afterward, Kingsley actually transforms into Cannon.

Remembering that his arch-rival, rackets boss Eric Marnay (Lugosi), was the one who tried to kill him, Cannon murders the members of Marnay's gang one by one. Not long afterward, Cannon retrieves the hidden money and disposes of Marnay by suffocating the rival gangster in a locked closet. Cannon then changes back into Kingsley, who has no recollection of the events, and Sovac rejoices at the prospect of using the

$500,000 to build a new research lab. Several months later, however, Kingsley unexpectedly changes into Cannon again during a class at the university. Believing that Sovac's daughter has the stolen money, Cannon tries to strangle her and Sovac is forced to kill him. Tried for murder, Sovac is sent to the electric chair, leaving behind a diary of the fantastic episode.

Black Friday turned out to be the last Karloff–Lugosi film for Universal, although the pair did team again at RKO in the mid-forties for the classic Val Lewton film, *The Body Snatcher.*

Bela Lugosi, Anne Nagel

EACH DAWN I DIE

A WARNER BROTHERS PICTURE.   1940

James Cagney and George Raft

CREDITS

Directed by William Keighley. *Associate producer:* David Lewis. *Screenplay by* Norman Reilly Raine, Warren Duff and Charles Perry. *Director of photography:* Arthur Edeson. *Art direction:* Max Parker. *Film editor:* Thomas Richards. *Sound recording by* E. A. Brown. *Music score by* Max Steiner. *Musical director:* Leo F. Forbstein. *Costumes by* Howard Shoup. *Make-up by* Perc Westmore. *Assistant director:* Frank Heath. *Running time:* 92 minutes.

CAST

Frank Ross: James Cagney; *Hood Stacey:* George Raft; *Joyce Conover:* Jane Bryan; *Warden Armstrong:* George Bancroft; *Fargo Red:* Maxie Rosenbloom; *Mueller:* Stanley Ridges; *Pole Cat:* Alan Baxter; *Grayce:* Victor Jory; *Pete Kassock:* John Wray; *Dale:* Edward Pawley; *Mrs. Ross:* Emma Dunn; *Garsky:* Paul Hurst; *Limpy:* Joe Downing.

Each Dawn I Die rates a special place in gangster film history for two reasons. It represents the only time that James Cagney and George Raft appeared as a screen team, and it was Cagney's temporary farewell to the genre. Released in 1940, it was the last gangster picture Cagney made until the release of *White Heat* nearly ten years later.

97

Victor Jory (*1. standing*) and James Cagney

James Cagney and James Flavin

James Cagney, Jane Bryan, John Ridgely

Stuart Holmes and James Cagney

James Cagney and George Bancroft

as compelling as when he breaks down sobbing in front of a parole board that has just rejected his plea for a pardon. The real gangster in *Each Dawn I Die* was George Raft, who also enjoyed one of his finest hours as the aptly named "Hood" Stacey, a slick rackets boss who befriends Cagney and eventually clears him. Cagney and Raft worked well together, and their many scenes had a realistic aura of affection and comraderie that enhanced their characterizations.

Interestingly, *Each Dawn I Die* was to have co-starred one of Cagney's favorite leading ladies, Ann Sheridan, as his love interest, but, for a variety of reasons, she ended up being replaced by newcomer Jane Bryan, who turned in a fine performance. *Each Dawn I Die* boasted excellent supporting performances from George Bancroft as the stern but compassionate warden, and Stanley Ridges as an inmate driven to the breaking point by a sadistic guard.

SYNOPSIS

Cagney is Frank Ross, a young newspaperman who wants to expose the corruption within the district attorney's office. He obtains several bits of damning evidence concerning the D. A.'s link to a crooked construction company, and when he writes a brilliant exposé of this, the D. A.'s henchmen hire a group of strong-arm criminals to try and stop Frank. Since they know that murdering the young reporter would be far too risky, they decide instead to frame him for a serious crime. While leaving his office at the newspaper one evening, Frank is bludgeoned by the thugs and rendered unconscious. The hoods carry Frank to his car and sit him behind the steering wheel, then douse the helpless newsman and the entire front seat with two quarts of liquor. Jamming the accelerator, the mobsters launch Frank's car on a deadly course down the main street of town, where it collides horribly with another vehicle, resulting in the deaths of an innocent family.

Frank is tried and convicted of manslaughter, and subsequently sentenced to prison, despite the fact that his friends at the newspaper launch an all-out effort to prove he was framed. During his stay at the Big House, Ross befriends "Hood"

Throughout most of the forties, Cagney made a conscious effort to steer clear of crime dramas, which he was afraid might type cast him. In fact, he fully intended that *Each Dawn I Die* serve as his official retirement from films of this kind, but he was lured back in 1949 by the superbly written and challenging script for *White Heat*. Though *Each Dawn I Die* remains somewhat overshadowed by better known films like *Little Caesar, The Public Enemy* and *G-Men*, the picture gave Cagney one of his meatiest and most intense roles, which he played to the absolute hilt.

Cagney appears as an ambitious, hardworking newspaper reporter who is framed on a manslaughter charge and sent to prison; he soon develops a criminal mentality as a result of his daily contact with thugs. The film gave Cagney several powerful scenes, and he has seldom been

Stacey (George Raft), a racketeer who promises to clear Frank by finding the men who framed him if Ross agrees to help him escape. Together, they engineer a daring plan that enables Stacey to flee from custody and check his underworld sources to learn the identities of the men who set Frank up. Stacey manages to obtain the necessary evidence to clear Frank, but is arrested and sent back to prison. At Sing Sing, however, Stacey presents the evidence to the warden (George Bancroft), who then takes the necessary action to get Frank released.

Each Dawn I Die was both a critical and commercial success, and many reviews pointed up the fact that Cagney and Raft made a truly splendid screen team. Through their excellent ability to play off one another, the stars managed to transform the rather average script into something memorable.

Charles Trowbridge, Victor Jory, James Cagney

JOHNNY APOLLO

A 20TH CENTURY-FOX PICTURE.   1940

Marc Lawrence, Lloyd Nolan, Tyrone Power, Edward Arnold

CREDITS

Directed by Henry Hathaway. *Associate producer:* Harry Joe Brown. *Screenplay by* Philip Dunne and Rowland Brown. *Original story by* Samuel G. Engel and Hal Long. *Director of photography:* Arthur Miller. *Art direction:* Richard Day and Wiard B. Ihnen. *Set decorations:* Thomas Little. *Film editor:* Robert Bischoff. *Costumes:* Gwen Wakeling. *Sound by* E. Clayton Ward and Roger Heman. *Musical direction:* Cyril J. Mockeridge. *In charge of production:* Darryl F. Zanuck. *Running time:* 96 minutes.

CAST

Bob Cain: Tyrone Power; *"Lucky" Dubarry:* Dorothy Lamour; *Robert Cain, Sr.:* Edward Arnold; *Mickey Dwyer:* Lloyd Nolan; *Jim McLaughlin:* Lionel Atwill; *Judge Brennan:* Charley Grapewin; *Bates:* Marc Lawrence; *Dr. Brown:* Jonathan Hale; *Piano Player:* Harry Rosenthal; *District Attorney:* Russell Hicks; *Cell Mate:* Fuzzy Knight; *Assistant D.A.:* Charles Lane; *Warden:* Selmar Jackson; *Judge:* Charles Trowbridge; *Judge:* John Hamilton; *Paul:* William Pawley; *Butler:* Eric Wilton.

Twentieth Century-Fox, a studio noted primarily for lavish Technicolor musicals and big-budget

"prestige" pictures such as *Lloyds of London,*
Alexander's Ragtime Band and *Jesse James,*
surprised the industry when, in 1940, it produced
a rather grim, hard-boiled crime drama called
Johnny Apollo, which starred, of all people, Tyrone
Power in his first and only gangster role. Unlike
some of the other studios, who shamelessly copied
the Warner Brothers format in their contributions
to the genre, Fox gave *Johnny Apollo* an entirely
fresh and original interpretation. The character
played by Power was in no way similar to the
Warners gangsters but was a suave, college-
educated young man from a well-to-do family, who
falls into the rackets almost by accident.

As a further departure from tradition, Fox cast
the popular musical star Dorothy Lamour, known
primarily for lightweight tropical romances (and
later for the famous *Road* series with Bing Crosby
and Bob Hope) in one of her rare dramatic outings

Lloyd Nolan and Tyrone Power

Edward Arnold and Tyrone Power

Tyrone Power and Dorothy Lamour

singer nor a dancer. The third and most obvious choice was Alice Faye, Fox's number-one musical star who had also worked with Power before and who could sing, dance *and* act. Faye was bound by other commitments, however, and Fox ended up borrowing Lamour from Paramount. The potent combination of the handsome Power and the sexy, pouting Lamour succeeded in winning audiences over, although *Johnny Apollo* turned out to be both their first and last film together.

SYNOPSIS

Robert Cain, Sr. (Edward Arnold), a prominent stockbroker, is arrested for embezzlement. Know-

as the nightclub singer moll of the rackets boss (played by Lloyd Nolan) who hires Power as his right-hand man. Though Lamour was splendid in the part, she was, amazingly enough, the studio's fourth choice for the role. Fox originally wanted to co-star Power with Linda Darnell, who had appeared with the actor a number of times previously but, because she lacked the musical talent that was essential to the character, she was never officially cast. Fox's second choice was the superb actress Nancy Kelly (who had played opposite Power the year before in *Jesse James*), who would have doubtless worked wonders with the dramatic interludes, but who, like Darnell, was neither a ing it will be a tough rap to beat, Cain hires the best defense attorney in the business, Jim McLaughlin (Lionel Atwill), to try and get him off the hook. Despite the lawyer's brilliant defense strategy, however, the evidence against Cain is simply too strong, and he is subsequently convicted and sent to prison. When this happens, his son, Bob Jr. (Power), is forced to abandon his college studies and return home so that he can aid in the effort to get his father released. Bob goes to see Judge Brennan (Charley Grapewin) who, it is rumored in the criminal underworld, will obtain paroles for prisoners if their families are able to meet his price. Through his association with Brennan, Bob meets mobster Mickey Dwyer (Lloyd Nolan) and his mistress "Lucky" DuBarry (Lamour), and soon becomes a member of Dwyer's gang, taking the flashy alias Johnny Apollo. Later, he and Lucky fall in love and begin a clandestine romance behind Mickey's back.

Through his activity in the rackets, Bob soon saves enough money to finance his father's parole, but before he is able to pay Brennan off, the judge is assassinated by gangsters. Later on, Bob and Mickey are arrested and sent to the same prison as the elder Cain, who, as it turns out, now wants nothing to do with his son because of his involvement with the rackets. Meanwhile, Dwyer engineers an escape plan for himself and Bob, and when Lucky learns of this, she communicates with Cain Sr., imploring him to discourage his son from going with Dwyer. When the elder Cain tries to do this, however, he is shot by Dwyer, who then knocks Bob out and plants the murder weapon next to him. Dwyer is killed during the ensuing escape attempt, and Bob is cleared of an attempted murder charge when Cain Sr. recovers and tells police it was Dwyer, not his son, who tried to kill him.

Johnny Apollo was excellently directed by Henry Hathaway, who managed to draw from Power a strong, convincing performance that was truly the most striking element in the picture, despite the fact that the actor was playing against such veteran scene-stealers as Edward Arnold, Lionel Atwill and Charley Grapewin. The combination of Power and Hathaway yielded such top-quality results that they joined forces on four more films, all of which were successful.

Dorothy Lamour

105

HIGH SIERRA

A WARNER BROTHERS PICTURE.   1941

Humphrey Bogart and Ida Lupino

Ida Lupino and Humphrey Bogart

CREDITS

Directed by Raoul Walsh. *Executive producer:* Hal B. Wallis. *Associate producer:* Mark Hellinger. *Screenplay by* John Huston and W. R. Burnett. *Based on the novel by* W. R. Burnett. *Director of photography:* Tony Gaudio. *Film editor:* Jack Killifer. *Music by* Adolph Deutsch. *Dialogue director:* Irving Rapper. *Art direction:* Ted Smith. *Gowns by* Milo Anderson. *Make-up by* Perc Westmore. *Sound recording by* Dolph Thomas. *Running time:* 100 minutes.

CAST

Roy Earle: Humphrey Bogart; *Marie Garson:* Ida Lupino; *Red:* Arthur Kennedy; *Babe:* Alan Curtis; *Velma:* Joan Leslie; *Doc Banton:* Henry Hull; *Pa Goodhue:* Henry Travers; *Healy:* Jerome Cowan; *Kranmer:* Barton MacLane; *Ma Goodhue:* Elisabeth Risdon; *Louie Mendoza:* Cornel Wilde; *Big Mack:* Donald MacBride; *Algernon:* Willie Best.

Despite the fact that he had been working in films since 1930, Humphrey Bogart did not achieve stardom until the forties, when such pictures as *The Maltese Falcon, Casablanca* and

He knew he'd be killed! But what about his dreams? A fireside, a farm, a woman's arms? What about the dime-a-dance dame he was good to? What made him an enemy of the people...and put a gun in his hand instead of a plow? The answer can only be told by...

IDA
LUPINO

Taxi-dancer, gun-moll, hungry-hearted woman! Greater than she was in "They Drive By Night"!

HUMPHREY
BOGART

In the strange, brooding figure of Roy Earle, he finds his greatest role!

IDA
LUPINO
HUMPHREY
BOGART

RAOUL WALSH

No Man Ever Reached
Greater Heights...
TO WAIT FOR DEATH!

Treasure of the Sierra Madre made him one of the top box office attractions of the decade. Bogart had spent most of the thirties playing an astonishing number of supporting villains in the big-budget gangster epics starring Robinson and Cagney, and in almost every one of them, Bogart as the treacherous heavy met a violent and bloody death. Though the black-hearted racketeers Bogart portrayed in these films were one-dimensional, to say the least, they usually provided the actor the chance to play a dramatic death scene at the climax of the story, in which he was allowed to briefly display the talent that would later make him Warner Brothers' number-one male star. These scenes were, for Bogart, isolated moments of glory in what were otherwise routine roles, as they were dramatically lit for maximum impact, underscored by swelling crescendos from Max Steiner's orchestra, and featured Bogart's bad guy

uttering a cynical farewell speech that was often quite poignant and powerful.

Bogart's wide experience with the genre made it somewhat fitting that his first starring role in a major class "A" production was that of a gangster, Roy "Mad Dog" Earle, in the 1941 classic *High Sierra*. Though it is now difficult to imagine anyone else as the modern-day desperado who feels that fate is closing in on him, Bogart was far from Warners' first choice for the role. The part was offered first to Cagney, then to Robinson, but both actors refused it because, by 1941, they were seeking to escape their gangster images and move on to other things. The studio's third choice was the popular George Raft, who also balked, supposedly on the grounds that he would never consent to portray a character whom the script required to die on screen. Hence, the role was awarded to Bogart simply because none of the

Ida Lupino

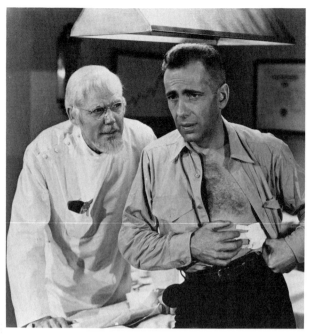

Henry Hull and Humphrey Bogart

more established stars wanted to play it, and he managed to deliver a splendid performance as the aging, doomed gangster.

The character Roy Earle was a distinct departure from the slick, big-city underworld types that Bogart had played throughout the thirties, and was more of a modern-day outlaw à la John Dillinger and Clyde Barrow, who used crime as a means of survival. Bogart's portrayal was uniformly praised by critics, and audiences flocked to the thrilling gangster saga in droves, proving once and for all that Bogart had the box office pull of a major star.

SYNOPSIS

Roy Earle (Bogart), one of the last of the old-time gangsters, is released from prison after 15 years. Driving to a remote cabin in the Sierra

Arthur Kennedy and Humphrey Bogart

Humphrey Bogart
and Ida Lupino

Nevada mountains, Roy meets with Red (Arthur Kennedy) and Babe (Alan Curtis), two young hoodlums hired by Roy's former boss, rackets chief Big Mack (Donald McBride), to pull off a daring robbery of the lush El Tropico resort in California. Though the young hoods respect Roy and obey him, they continually come to blows over Marie Garson (Ida Lupino), a girl they picked up in Los Angeles. When Earle orders her to leave, she implores him to reconsider, and, not long afterward, she becomes infatuated with the aging criminal.

Meanwhile, Roy befriends Mr. and Mrs. Goodhue (Elizabeth Risdon and Henry Travers) and their granddaughter Velma (Joan Leslie), a beautiful young woman who suffers from a club foot. Falling in love with Velma, Roy offers to finance surgery that will correct her deformity, and confesses to Mr. Goodhue that he hopes, more than anything else, that Velma will consent to marry him. When Velma's operation is successful, however, she vows to make up for her life of heartbreak and starts partying almost every night with her new boyfriend, a slick hustler named Lon (John Eldredge). When Roy proposes marriage, Velma rejects him, explaining that, despite all he has done for her, she simply doesn't love him. Deeply hurt by this, Roy turns to Marie for comfort. At last realizing that the tough but tender-

hearted Marie is more his kind, he falls in love with her.

Later, Red and Babe are killed in the aftermath of the El Tropico heist, leaving Roy to fence the lucrative take by himself. Going to Big Mack's apartment, Roy is saddened to find the old gangleader dead of heart failure. Learning that the police have instituted an all-out manhunt to capture him, Roy separates from Marie, promising to join her in Reno as soon as things cool down. While driving through a small town sometime afterward, however, Roy is spotted by a pair of rural cops, who radio the local sheriff's department. Pursued by a squad of police in cars and on motorcycles, Roy drives up the treacherous, winding roads of the high Sierra, taking refuge in the vast mountain range around nightfall. Roy is shot and killed by the law officers, but not before writing a small note that clears Marie of any involvement with his crimes.

High Sierra, aside from being Humphrey Bogart's first important star vehicle, is also noteworthy in that it was the second of three classic gangster films directed by Raoul Walsh. The director had previously displayed his flair for the genre with the excellent *The Roaring Twenties*, released the previous year, and would later direct James Cagney in the superb *White Heat* (1949).

111

JOHNNY EAGER

A METRO-GOLDWYN-MAYER PICTURE.   1941

Robert Taylor, Charles Dingle, Paul Stewart

112

Robert Taylor and Lana Turner

CREDITS

Directed by Mervyn LeRoy. *Produced by* John W. Considine. *Screenplay by* James Edward Grant and John Lee Mahin. *Director of photography:* Harold Rosson. *Film editor:* Albert Akst. *Running time:* 107 minutes.

CAST

Johnny Eager: Robert Taylor; *Lisbeth Bard:* Lana Turner; *John Benson Farrell:* Edward Arnold; *Jeff Hartnett:* Van Heflin; *Jimmy Courtney:* Robert Sterling; *Garnet:* Patricia Dane; *Mae Blythe:* Glenda Farrell; *Mr. Verne:* Henry O'Neill; *Judy Janford:* Diana Lewis; *Lew Rankin:* Barry Nelson; *Marco:* Charles Dingle; *Julio:* Paul Stewart; *Halligan:* Cy Kendall; *Billiken:* Don Costello; *Peg:* Connie Gilchrist; *Ryan:* Joseph Downing.

MGM, by far the richest and most powerful of all the studios, had been one of the most prolific film factories of the thirties. Curiously, however, the company had neglected both the gangster and the horror film genres throughout the decade, despite the fact that both had proven immensely lucrative for Warner Brothers and Universal. All this changed, however, in 1941, when MGM invested its considerable resources in the mounting of one opulent, beautifully produced example of each. Their horror film was a big-budget remake of *Dr. Jekyll and Mr. Hyde,* starring Spencer Tracy and Ingrid Bergman, and their entry into the gangster film derby was *Johnny Eager,* starring Robert Taylor and Lana Turner. The deluxe, streamlined gangster flick proved the more popular of the two, and emerged as one of MGM's most successful movies of the year.

Robert Taylor, MGM's handsomest and most adored matinee idol, may have seemed an odd choice for a gangster role, but he managed to turn in an excellent performance as the high-living racketeer who is eventually brought down by love. Supposedly, the studio cast Taylor as the lead in *Johnny Eager* to squelch the notion that all he could play was pretty boy roles, and a viewing of the picture indeed reveals a conscious attempt to downplay his attractiveness. As Eager, Taylor sported a thin black mustache that made him look much older than his thirty years, and, throughout the drama, was outfitted in darkly colored suits and hats that made him appear more threatening

than appealing. MGM's attempt to prove that Taylor wasn't just another pretty face and was an actor of definite skill and range provided Taylor with one of his best and most atypical roles, although many critics remarked that he looked as handsome as ever and was really too good-looking to be convincing in this kind of part. The box office receipts proved different, however, as audiences welcomed the chance to see the dashing star play a cunning, despicable heel.

The film, though not quite as good as the best of the Warners classics, is still very enjoyable, containing the lush settings and beautiful, soft-edged black-and-white photography that were well-known trademarks of MGM during the forties. Moreover, *Johnny Eager* was directed by Mervyn LeRoy, who had engineered the first great sound gangster film, *Little Caesar,* and his expertise with the genre was evident throughout. MGM launched *Johnny Eager* with a strong publicity campaign, which promised that the studio's foray into the gangster genre was "pure TNT," which proved a clever way of capitalizing on the names of

Paul Stewart and Robert Taylor

Robert Taylor and Barry Nelson

its two stars. Van Heflin's excellent performance as Taylor's alcoholic friend Jeff won him an Academy Award for best supporting actor, making him the first performer to win an Oscar for a role in a gangster movie.

SYNOPSIS

Johnny Eager (Taylor), a high-living, big-city racketeer, operates his criminal dealings from a lavish penthouse apartment, which he shares with a friend, Jeff Hartnett (Heflin), a cynical drunkard whose specialty is amateur philosophy. During his travels around town one evening, Eager meets a

pretty socialite named Lisbeth Bard (Turner), who falls in love with him. Learning that she is the stepdaughter of the district attorney (Edward Arnold), who has been out to nail him for some time, Eager feigns a romantic interest in her while planning a dubious scheme to get the D. A. off his back. He engineers a fake homicide and convinces Lisbeth that she has killed a man, thus getting something on her that he can use as a tool against her stepfather. Somewhere down the line, however, Eager really falls for her and does a complete turnabout, telling her she did not really commit a murder, and even "introducing" her to the man she was supposed to have killed. Before the

115

Robert Taylor
and Henry O'Neill

Van Heflin and Robert Taylor

Robert Taylor

116

reformed gangster and the young society girl have a chance to build a new life, however, Eager is shot and killed by police.

Johnny Eager gave Turner one of her best and most challenging roles of the forties, and Edward Arnold's portrayal of the hard-nosed D. A. was also finely drawn.

OUT OF THE FOG

A WARNER BROTHERS PICTURE.   1941

Eddie Albert,
John Garfield, Ida Lupino

CREDITS

Directed by Anatole Litvak. *Executive producer:*
Hal B. Wallis. *Associate producer:* Henry Blanke.
Screenplay by Robert Rossen, Jerry Wald and
Richard Macaulay. From Irwin Shaw's play *The
Gentle People. Director of photography:* James
Wong Howe. *Art direction:* Carl Jules Weyl. *Film
editor:* Warren Low. *Special effects by* Rex Wimpy.
Music director: Leo F. Forbstein. *Running time:*
85 minutes.

CAST

Harold Goff: John Garfield; *Stella Goodwin:* Ida
Lupino; *George Watkins:* Eddie Albert; *Jonah
Goodwin:* Thomas Mitchell; *Olaf Johnson:* John

Ida Lupino and John Garfield

120

John Garfield, John Qualen, Eddie Albert,
Thomas Mitchell

Qualen; *Igor Propotkin:* George Tobias; *Florence
Goodwin:* Aline MacMahon; *District Attorney:*
Jerome Cowan; *Caroline Pomponette:* Odette
Myrtil; *Eddie:* Leo Gorcey; *Judge Moriarity:* Paul
Harvey; *Officer Magruder:* Robert Homans; *Sam
Pepper:* Bernard Gorcey; *Detective:* Charles
Wilson.

John Garfield's brief fling at Warners gangster
stardom ended with *Out of the Fog,* which was the
only one of the studio's classic crime films of the
forties based on a stage work. It was a faithful
adaptation of Irwin Shaw's play *The Gentle People,*
which told the story of a vicious petty gangster
who preys on a small group of down-and-outers
until they decide to fight back. Of his three
Warners gangster vehicles, Garfield probably
respected this one more than the others, not only
because of its stage origins, but also because the
property had been originally produced on Broadway by the Theatre Guild, an organization Garfield
no doubt had great admiration for. Released in
1941, *Out of the Fog* garnered the actor some of
the best notices of his career, many of them calling
his portrayal of Harold Goff, the small-time racke-

teer who lords it over the poor, his finest screen
acting thus far.

Out of the Fog was decidedly restrained for a
Warner Brothers gangster film: There were no
gangland shootouts or dramatic deathhouse
sequences, and the picture emerged as more of a
moody character study, a quiet, cerebral drama of
injustice and revenge. The setting for the story
was remarkably appropriate: a small seaside
village continually engulfed in an oppressive,
swirling fog, where the lives of the impoverished
but hard-working inhabitants are temporarily
disrupted by the coming, seemingly out of no-
where, of the evil gangster. The seaside town,
beautifully designed by Warners' ace art director
Carl Jules Weyl, with its turn of the century saloon
and its bleak, fog-laden docks, give the proceedings an almost dreamlike quality, and the village's
rather "Twilight Zonish" flavor added greatly to the
picture's atmosphere.

Veteran character actors Thomas Mitchell and
John Qualen were both outstanding as the two old
men who, after suffering several injustices at the
hands of the criminal, finally muster the courage
to take revenge, and Dead End Kid Leo Gorcey
also scored well as a young saloon worker. Interestingly enough, *Out of the Fog* turned out to be

Thomas Mitchell and John Garfield

Thomas Mitchell, Ida Lupino, John Garfield, Eddie Albert

the only Warners gangster drama in which the law was not ultimately upheld . . . the two old men plot, and eventually cause, albeit accidentally, the gangster's death. Incredibly, the local policeman, knowing full well what has taken place, decides to look the other way. This refreshing notion that a higher justice was allowed to prevail was quite remarkable in a forties film, and made *Out of the Fog* years ahead of its time in terms of attitude and moral stance.

SYNOPSIS

The story takes place in Sheepshead Bay, Brooklyn. Two elderly fishermen (Thomas Mitchell and John Qualen) earn a meager living from their small boat, and dream of one day buying a bigger craft so that their daily catch might be increased. Suddenly and unexpectedly, a small-time hoodlum, Harold Goff (Garfield), comes into town and terrorizes the populace by setting up a protection racket, in which he extorts what little money the townspeople have. Not surprisingly, Goff manages to scare the two old men into giving him their entire life savings. The young daughter (Ida Lupino) of one of the fisherman, discontented with her drab life and dreaming of an escape, is attracted to the young gangster and agrees to run away with him after he has bled the town dry. When her father tries to prevent the girl from seeing the criminal, Goff beats the old man up. Finally becoming angry at the ease with which the gangster has taken control of their lives, the two old men decide to kill him, and they manage to talk him into accompanying them on their boat, fully intending to push Goff overboard at the first opportunity. Realizing their plan and surprised that such passive souls would undertake such a drastic revenge, Goff becomes frightened and topples into the sea, drowning. Later, a policeman investigating the incident manages to guess the truth, but decides to do nothing about it.

Though Garfield made it known that he disliked appearing in gangster films, the actor would return to the genre several more times during his career. Indeed, his last screen role was as the desperate hood in 1951's *He Ran All the Way*.

124

THIS GUN FOR HIRE

A PARAMOUNT PICTURE.   1942

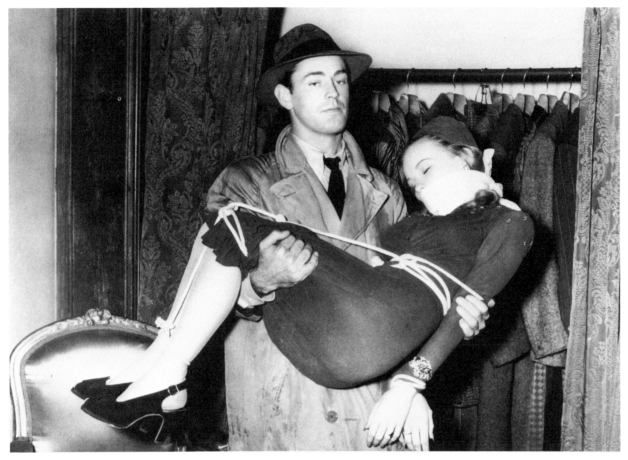

Alan Ladd and Veronica Lake

CREDITS

Directed by Frank Tuttle. *Produced by* Richard M. Blumenthal. *Screenplay by* Albert Maltz and W. R. Burnett. *Based on the novel by* Graham Greene. *Director of photography:* John Seitz. *Musical score by* David Buttolph. *Film editor:* Archie Marshek. *Running time:* 81 minutes.

CAST

Ellen Graham: Veronica Lake; *Raven:* Alan Ladd; *Willard Gates:* Laird Cregar; *Mike Crane:* Robert Preston; *Alvin Brewster:* Tully Marshall; *Sluky:* Mikhail Rasumny; *Tommy:* Marc Lawrence; *Annie:* Pamela Burke; *Albert Baker:* Frank Ferguson; *Senator Burnett:* Roger Imhof; *Ruby:* Patricia Farr; *Night Watchman:* James Farley.

Like Robinson, Bogart and Cagney, Alan Ladd made his first major impression on audiences in a gangster role, his unforgettable Raven in *This Gun for Hire*. Surprisingly, it was Ladd's 36th film; from 1932 to 1941, the actor had been one of the industry's busiest extras, appearing in dozens of pictures as little more than a handsome face in the crowd. The part of Raven, the aloof professional killer, made Ladd a star, and was the prelude to a long and distinguished career, but the actor had

125

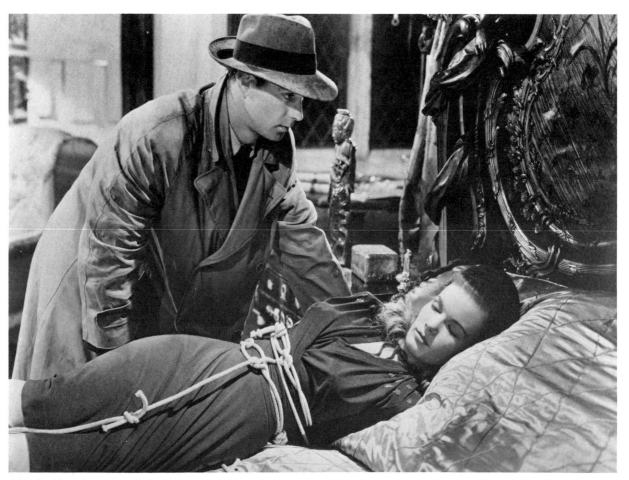

Alan Ladd and Veronica Lake

paid his dues in a long succession of bit parts before landing the role that made his name a household word. He can be glimpsed briefly in such diverse items as *Saturday's Millions* (1933), *Pigskin Parade* (1936), *The Goldwyn Follies* (1938), *The Green Hornet* (1940) and *In Old Missouri* (1940), and perhaps his most famous bit was as a newspaper reporter in *Citizen Kane* (1941). His first speaking parts of any distinction were in the Universal horror-comedy *The Black Cat* (1941) and the taut war thriller *Joan of Paris* (1942), but it wasn't until *This Gun For Hire* that Ladd finally came into his own. It was his first starring vehicle opposite Veronica Lake, who became his most frequent leading lady of the forties, and it established Ladd's screen image as a tough, uncompromising individualist.

Like Robinson's Little Caesar, Cagney's Rocky Sullivan and Bogart's Duke Mantee, Ladd's Raven remains one of the all-time great gangster charac-

terizations, a frightening yet strangely tragic figure who, despite his murderous ways, has a softer, more human side that the audience is allowed to glimpse briefly. The affection that Raven has for cats (whom he identifies with, because, in his own words, "they're on their own . . . they don't need nobody") and develops for Veronica Lake over the course of the story, makes the character all the more compelling to the audience. It is interesting to note that, unlike the three Warner Brothers stars who, following their star debuts in gangster roles, found themselves cast in a string of similar follow-up vehicles, Ladd never again played a bad guy on screen, and spent the remainder of his career portraying, for the most part, heroic characters and romantic leads. *This Gun For Hire* garnered the actor some of the best critical notices of his career, some of which praised his masterful handling of the role.

Laird Cregar, Marc Lawrence, Veronica Lake

Alan Ladd, Veronica Lake, Robert Preston

Laird Cregar, Marc Lawrence, Veronica Lake

128

SYNOPSIS

The story begins as Raven (Ladd) carries out a contract killing on two strangers that his employer, a corrupt, overweight millionaire named Willard Gates (Laird Cregar), wants out of the way. Following the murder, Raven meets with Gates to collect his fee. After paying the killer, Gates is overcome by curiousity as to how Raven feels when committing a murder. "I feel just fine," the killer assures him in cold, icy tones. Meanwhile, a United States Senator who suspects that Gates is involved in some sort of espionage, hires pretty Ellen Graham (Lake), the girlfriend of a tough L.A. cop, Mike Crane (Robert Preston), to do some undercover work. Posing as an ambitious singer, Ellen auditions for Gates and is hired to appear at his posh supper club. She soon discovers that the senator's suspicions are correct, and that Gates is indeed the front man for a gang of criminals who are selling poison gas to the enemy.

Later, Raven discovers that Gates paid him off in hot money and promises to kill the fat man in retaliation. Learning that Ellen is a spy working for the senator, Gates tries to have her eliminated at his home, but the vengeance-crazed Raven arrives just in time to prevent this. Gates manages to escape, and Raven decides to take Ellen as a kind of insurance policy against any police interference. Still wanting to kill Gates for double-crossing him, Raven sneaks into the factory where Gates and his cohorts carry out their espionage deals. Once inside, Raven kills Gates, several members of his gang, and the aging criminal mastermind Alvin Brewster (Tully Marshall), who is the brains behind it all. Having grown somewhat fond of Ellen, Raven decides to let her go, after which he is gunned down by police.

Ladd received excellent support in *This Gun for Hire,* especially from Laird Cregar as the corpulant crime mogul Willard Gates. Cregar's characterization was brilliant, and the priceless shot of the prissy fat man sitting up in bed reading *Paris Nights* while devouring chocolate bon-bons gave the grim crime drama its one humorous touch.

THE BIG SHOT

A WARNER BROTHERS PICTURE.   1942

Irene Manning and Humphrey Bogart

CREDITS

Directed by Lewis Seiler. *Produced by* Walter
MacEwen. *Screenplay by* Bertram Millhauser,
Abem Finkel and Daniel Fuchs. *Director of
photography:* Sid Hickox. *Music by* Adolph
Deutsch. *Film editor:* Jack Killifer. *Dialogue
director:* Harold Winston. *Assistant director:* Art
Lueker. *Art direction:* John Hughes. *Gowns by*
Milo Anderson. *Make-up by* Perc Westmore.
Sound recording by Stanley Jones. *Running time:*
82 minutes.

CAST

Duke Berne: Humphrey Bogart; *Lorna Fleming:*
Irene Manning; *George Anderson:* Richard Travis;
Ruth Carter: Susan Peters; *Martin Fleming:*
Stanley Ridges; *Warden Booth:* Minor Watson;
Dancer: Chick Chandler; *Frenchy:* Joseph Down-
ing; *Sandor:* Howard Da Silva; *Quinto:* Murray
Alper; *Faye:* Roland Drew; *Tim:* John Ridgely;
Judge: John Hamilton.

The Big Shot is an interesting curiosity in the
career of Humphrey Bogart. Though produced in
1942, the year after Bogart attained major stardom
with his appearance as Sam Spade in *The Maltese
Falcon*, the film is very reminiscent of the "B"
gangster pictures that the actor became famous
for during the thirties. Quickly produced on a
minimal budget, *The Big Shot* hardly seemed the
type of vehicle in which a rising superstar would

Humphrey Bogart and Irene Manning

Humphrey Bogart, Joseph Downing, Irene Manning

appear, and it pales in comparison to the other films that Bogart made during this period. When one remembers that *Across the Pacific*, *Casablanca* and *Sahara* were all produced around the same time as *The Big Shot*, the minor gangster drama seems oddly out of place amid such clas-

Humphrey Bogart and Richard Travis

by Bertram Millhauser, Abem Finkel and Daniel Fuchs and the decidedly offbeat casting of the regally beautiful Irene Manning as Bogart's moll.

The character Bogart played in *The Big Shot*—Duke Berne—was very similar to his classic Roy Earle of two years before, and the story's situations were also highly reminiscent of the earlier gangster picture, making *The Big Shot* a kind of poor man's *High Sierra*. Once again, Bogart appeared as an aging veteran gangster who plans one last heist on which to retire, and who is loved by a tough but tender-hearted woman who becomes an accessory to his crimes. As if the writers were truly trying to recreate the feel of *High Sierra*, there were several scenes that contained an almost identical look and style, and there was even a lengthy car chase through winding mountain roads, in which the police pursue the fugitive Duke Berne along what appears to be precisely the same route taken by Roy Earle. However, if one is willing to overlook the obvious similarities to Bogart's 1941 hit, then *The Big Shot* emerges as a taut, exciting mini-gangster epic, offering Bogart a fairly well-defined character, albeit of the type he had played dozens of times already.

sics. Though entertaining and well made, it is scarcely more than a second feature, and one wonders why Bogart agreed to appear in this throwback to his old gangster days when he was obviously moving on to bigger things. In the picture's favor, however, were a fairly good script

133

Irene Manning and Humphrey Bogart

SYNOPSIS

Duke Berne (Bogart), a seasoned criminal with many years of prison life behind him, plans to pull off an armored car robbery with several of his old gangster pals, who now take orders from a crooked attorney, Martin Fleming (Stanley Ridges). Berne learns that Fleming has not only taken control of his gang, but has also married Duke's former girlfriend, Lorna (Irene Manning). Duke visits her and finds that she still loves him and wants to divorce Fleming, who mistreats her. Wanting a fresh start with Duke that will include no criminal activity of any kind, she prevents him from taking part in the armored car heist by holding him at gunpoint in his room.

As it turns out, Duke's boys manage to pull the job off without him, but, sometime afterward, a witness mistakenly names Berne as one of the robbers and he is arrested. Duke's good friend George Anderson (Richard Travis) agrees to testify that Berne was with him during the robbery, but

Fleming nails him for perjury and both George and Duke are sent to prison. Later, Duke escapes from custody and is reunited with Lorna, and the two live happily for a time in a remote mountain cabin. Not long afterward, however, they are spotted by police, who pursue the fugitive couple along hazardous mountain roads. Lorna is killed during the chase, and Duke is later shot to death in a confrontation with Fleming.

Like so many of his earlier gangster movies, *The Big Shot* provided Bogart with still another dramatic death scene (during which the mortally wounded Berne requests a last cigarette) as well as a violent encounter with a hated enemy (this time the underhanded lawyer played by Stanley Ridges), after which Bogart and his adversary find themselves, as always, riddled with bullets. Incidentally, *The Big Shot* was Bogart's last gangster film until 1951, when he made a spectacular comeback to the genre as the crime-smashing district attorney in *The Enforcer*.

134

Humphrey Bogart and Irene Manning

THE GLASS KEY

A PARAMOUNT PICTURE.   1942

Alan Ladd and Margaret Heyes

CREDITS

Directed by Stuart Heisler. *Produced by* Fred Kohlmar. *Screenplay by* Jonathan Latimer. *From a novel by* Dashiell Hammett. *Director of photography:* Theodor Sparkuhl. *Film editor:* Archie Marshek. *Music by* Victor Young. *Running time:* 85 minutes.

CAST

Ed Beaumont: Alan Ladd; *Janet Henry:* Veronica Lake; *Paul Madvig:* Brian Donlevy; *Opal:* Bonita Granville; *Taylor Henry:* Richard Denning; *Nick Varna:* Joseph Calleia; *Jeff:* William Bendix;

Nurse: Frances Gifford; *Farr:* Donald MacBride; *Eloise Matthews:* Margaret Hayes; *Senator Henry:* Moroni Olsen; *Clyde Matthews:* Arthur Loft; *Rusty:* Eddie Marr.

Alan Ladd's second starring vehicle for Paramount was a remake of Dashiell Hammett's *The Glass Key,* which had originally been filmed in 1935 with George Raft. Even before *This Gun for Hire* had played its early engagements, the studio realized, after seeing the rushes, that it would probably make Ladd the screen sensation of the year. Knowing that they had found a truly bankable personality in the actor, they rushed him into this somber drama of gangsters and political intrigue. Curiously enough, Paramount, as yet unaware of the special screen chemistry of Ladd and Veronica Lake, initially cast Patricia Morison as the female lead in *The Glass Key,* but the early rushes revealed she was far too tall to play opposite the diminutive Ladd. In an emergency move, Lake

Brian Donlevy, Veronica Lake, Alan Ladd

138

was given the part, simply because she was shorter than Morison.

As a novel, *The Glass Key* was a very typical Hammett adventure, a tough, contemporary mystery featuring well-drawn but generally unsympathetic characters (in this respect, it was a great deal like *The Maltese Falcon*, perhaps the author's most famous work). This 1942 version, directed by Stuart Heisler, was in that sense faithful to the book, even more so than the earlier George Raft film, and emerged as a bleak, uncompromising drama filled with rather humorless, predatory characters.

The roles Ladd and Lake essayed in *The Glass Key* were, in a sense, less appealing than those they portrayed in *This Gun for Hire*. Raven, despite the fact that he was a criminal, and Ellen Graham each had brief moments of tenderness and pathos, which allowed the audience to really care about them, but the people they played in *The Glass Key* were another matter entirely. Lake appeared as a scheming, manipulative woman and

Alan Ladd and Donald MacBride

Joseph Calleia, William Bendix, Brian Donlevy, Alan Ladd

Ladd played a cynical opportunist, both of whom use political boss Brian Donlevy's affection for their own selfish gain. Despite the rather hard-hearted natures of their characters, however, audiences again responded strongly to Ladd and Lake as a screen team, and *The Glass Key* became a box office smash.

The film marked Ladd's first appearance with William Bendix, who would become one of the actor's most frequent co-stars of the forties, usually playing Ladd's good-hearted sidekick. In this film, however, Bendix appeared as a sadistic gangster who, in several scenes, nearly beats Ladd to death. Bendix's performance in *The Glass Key* was one of the best of his career, convincingly portraying a truly frightening strongarm bully who, in his own words, "likes to beat up on guys," and his characterization was made even more effective because of his usually likable screen image.

SYNOPSIS

The picture featured Ladd as Ed Beaumont, the right-hand man of crooked political boss Paul Madvig (Brian Donlevy). Madvig is in love with attractive socialite Janet Henry (Lake), who has agreed to marry him if he backs her father, aging politician Ralph Henry (Moroni Olson), as a candidate for mayor. When Janet meets Ed, the attraction is immediate, and she begins flirting with the young aide behind Madvig's back. Meanwhile, Madvig objects to his kid sister Opal (Bonita Granville) carrying on a romance with Janet's no-good brother, Taylor (Richard Denning).

When Taylor is murdered some time later, Madvig becomes the prime suspect, and he orders Ed to try and find out who the real killer is. Nick Varna (Joseph Calleia), a powerful racketeer with political ambitions of his own, begins a smear campaign against Madvig. Failing to turn up anything tangible on Taylor's murder, Ed decides to investigate Varna, which proves a costly error, as he is beaten within an inch of his life by Jeff (William Bendix), Varna's bodyguard. Later, one of Varna's mob is murdered and the police arrest Madvig on circumstantial evidence, but he is later cleared when Ed manages to trick Jeff into confessing to the crime. Not long afterward, it is learned that Taylor was killed by his own father over a gambling debt, and, at last free of suspicion, Madvig resumes his political career. Realizing the attraction that Ed and Janet feel for each other, Madvig relinquishes his engagement to her, and gives the young couple his blessing as they depart for New York.

Brian Donlevy was excellent as the political boss, the role played by Edward Arnold in the 1935 film, and Richard Denning also had several good scenes as the spoiled, no-account rich boy who is murdered by his father.

THE KILLERS

A UNIVERSAL PICTURE.   1946

Vince Barnett and Edmund O'Brien

CREDITS

Directed by Robert Siodmak. *Produced by* Mark Hellinger. *Screenplay by* Anthony Veiller. *Based on a story by* Ernest Hemingway. *Director of photography:* Elwood Bredell. *Musical score by* Miklos Rozsa. *Running time:* 105 minutes.

CAST

Swede: Burt Lancaster; *Kitty:* Ava Gardner; *Riordan:* Edmund O'Brien; *Colfax:* Albert Dekker; *Lieutenant Lubinsky:* Sam Levene; *Blinky:* Jeff Corey; *Kenyon:* Donald MacBride; *Dum Dum:* Jack Lambert; *Charleston:* Vince Barnett; *Packy:* Charles D. Brown; *Lilly:* Virginia Christine; *The Killers:* William Conrad, Charles McGraw.

Ernest Hemingway's popular and widely read short story "The Killers," written in the 1920's, remains one of the author's most cleverly crafted works. It captivated readers with its bristling tension and suspense, and in 1946 it was made into a major motion picture by Universal, directed by Robert Siodmak and starring Burt Lancaster in the role that introduced him to the screen. Hemingway's story told of two hired killers who arrive in a small town and wait in the local diner for their "hit," a nameless down-and-outer living in

141

Burt Lancaster and Ava Gardner

142

a dingy rented room. The story's effectiveness was enhanced by the fact that Hemingway provided no explanation as to who any of the men were or why one of them had to die. In its original form, the rather brief story would no doubt have made an excellent "Playhouse 90" or "Twilight Zone" television drama, but there simply wasn't enough material for a feature-length film.

Universal, after securing the rights to the story, hired screenwriter Anthony Veiller to expand on the story by inventing histories for the characters and imagining what events might have led up to the fatal rendezvous. As it turned out, the studio got more than they bargained for, as Veiller fashioned a brilliant script that included elements of crime, betrayal and sexual obsession, and added a string of fascinating new characters. The scenes based on the Hemingway story appeared at the beginning of the movie, with Veiller's embellish-

ments then neatly unfolding into a long flashback. The audience learns that the doomed man was once a top-ranking professional fighter, whose involvement with gangsters and a beautiful, treacherous woman has caused his downfall, and whose betrayal of the criminals is the reason for his impending death.

Lancaster was, of course, wonderful as the unfortunate young boxer, Swede, and few actors have had a more forceful or impressive debut (although it was technically Lancaster's second film; he had, the year before, appeared in a picture for Paramount called *Desert Fury* which the studio, in a curious move, reportedly deemed a rather flat vehicle for the powerful new star, and shelved until the release of this much more impressive Universal film). Albert Dekker cut a truly menacing figure as the racketeer who takes over Lancaster's life, and Ava Gardner has never

Edmund O'Brien and Perc Launders

143

Burt Lancaster (*in ring*) and Sam Levene

been better than as Kitty Collins, the femme fatale who plays a key role in Lancaster's destruction. And among the most memorable scenes in the picture were the early ones revolving around the two killers, played with icy calm by Charles McGraw and William Conrad.

SYNOPSIS

Two mysterious men (McGraw and Conrad) arrive in a small town one night and decide to pass the evening at the local diner. Their menacing tone and manner soon makes it apparent that they are not ordinary customers, and are probably there for some dubious purpose. They engage in taunting, abusive banter with the mild-mannered owner (Harry Hayden), calling him "bright boy" and ordering him to refuse any more customers for the remainder of the evening. They then ask the owner to confirm that a man known as Swede (Lancaster) comes into the diner every night around seven, and, when they are told he does, they freely admit that they are there to murder him. Several blocks away, in a run-down hotel, Swede waits pensively in a dingy room, knowing

Sam Levene and Edmund O'Brien

146

Jack Lambert (*atop roof*)

that the killers have come to get him and completely resigned to his fate.

A flashback reveals that Swede has been, for most of his life, a man cursed by bad luck. He was once an up and coming middleweight, who lost the most important bout of his career because he was forced to fight with an injured hand. Shortly after his loss in the ring, Swede had become involved with the beautiful Kitty Collins (Gardner), who initially seemed the perfect girl for him but who, once she had the fighter hooked, insisted that he join the gang of a powerful racketeer, Colfax (Dekker). Complying with Kitty's wish, Swede assisted the gangsters in a daring robbery, but eventually betrayed them, resulting in a contract being placed on his life. Despite their lucrative haul from the heist, Colfax's gang began mistrusting one another, which led to a bloody shootout in which most of them were killed. Swede managed to escape his enslavement to Colfax and the girl, going far away to the small town, where he was hired as a filling station attendant. The scene then shifts back to the sleazy hotel room, where Swede meets his death at the hands of the killers.

The Killers was allegedly the only screen adaptation of a Hemingway work that the author actually liked. It was later remade by Universal in 1964 as a star vehicle for Lee Marvin and Ronald Reagan.

Edmund O'Brien

OUT OF THE PAST

An RKO RADIO PICTURE.   1947

Robert Mitchum, Paul Valentine, Ken Miles

CREDITS

Directed by Jacques Tourneur. *Produced by* Warren Duff. *Screenplay by* Geoffrey Homes. *Director of photography:* Nicholas Musuraca. *Film editor:* Samuel E. Beetley. *Art directors:* Albert S. D'Agostino and Jack Okey. *Musical score by* Roy Webb. *Running time:* 97 minutes.

CAST

Jeff: Robert Mitchum; *Kathie:* Jane Greer; *Whit:* Kirk Douglas; *Meta Carson:* Rhonda Fleming; *Joe Stefanos:* Paul Valentine; *Jim:* Richard Webb; *Fisher:* Steve Brodie; *Ann:* Virginia Huston; *Eels:* Ken Miles; *The Kid:* Dickie Moore.

The late forties saw a definite change in several classic film genres, most notably the horror film, the western and the gangster picture. The movies were becoming increasingly "psychological" in tone, and the stories and characters were far more complex than they had been in the previous decade. For instance, the superb series of horror films produced by Universal, with their emphasis on elaborate castle and graveyard settings and grotesque monster make-ups, had, by the mid-

Paul Valentine, Kirk Douglas, Robert Mitchum

Jane Greer, Robert Mitchum, Steve Brodie

forties, run their course, and were being replaced by the subtler, more cerebral chills of the Val Lewton horror pictures being produced at RKO. The rough and tumble, action-packed westerns of the thirties and early forties, with their rather simple good-guys-versus-bad-guys plots, were likewise giving way to westerns that were rife with symbolism and Freudian overtones, such as the excellent *Pursued* (1947), directed by Raoul Walsh and starring Robert Mitchum.

So, too, the gangster films of the era displayed a similar turning away from the black-and-white villains and heroes of the Robinson–Cagney–Bogart era, and a tendency toward characters of more depth and complexity. The protagonists in these films were a far cry from the "larger than life" gangsters of the Warners era, and were often depicted as ordinary men who, due to some dark, hidden facet of their personality, were drawn to crime almost like a moth to flame, knowing it would mean their destruction but still unable to resist.

One of the finest examples of this new breed of gangster films was *Out of the Past*, released in 1947 and featuring an entire new generation of stars who, at the time, were just beginning to make their mark in motion pictures. Robert Mitchum, Kirk Douglas, Jane Greer and Rhonda

Steve Brodie, Jane Greer, Robert Mitchum

Kirk Douglas and Robert Mitchum

Fleming were all on their way to bright movie careers, and *Out of the Past* featured these stars in one of the finest of their early works. Mitchum appeared as a private detective who is hired by a big-time gangster (Douglas) to find Douglas's vanished mistress, played by Greer. While tailing the elusive beauty, Mitchum meets and falls in love with her and double-crosses Douglas, then plunges deeper and deeper into a tangled web of corruption.

Containing excellent performances from all concerned, *Out of the Past* was an especially fine showcase for Kirk Douglas, who played Whit Sterling, a wealthy racketeer. Despite his criminal ways, Sterling enjoys the finer things in life and is a man of refinement and culture, a far cry from the crude crime bosses portrayed in the gangster films of the thirties. Likewise, the character played by Greer was also a new breed of gangster's moll, hardly the goodtime flapper type of the earlier

Warner films, but a deadly seductress, beautiful and irresistible, but evil to the core.

SYNOPSIS

The story begins in a small town, where Jeff (Mitchum), who runs the local filling station, leads a quiet, uneventful life in the hope of forever burying his sordid past. One day, however, he is visited by Joe Stefanos (Paul Valentine), the right-hand man of mobster Whit Sterling (Douglas), whom Jeff once worked for. Stefanos orders Jeff to report to Sterling for another "assignment" and, knowing it might prove fatal to refuse, Jeff complies.

On his way to Sterling's mountain retreat, Jeff, in a flashback, remembers his past involvement with the gangster. Whit had hired Jeff, then a private investigator, to find his mistress Kathie (Greer), who had vanished with $40,000 of Whit's money. Finding the girl in Mexico, Jeff fell in love with her himself, and decided to betray Whit and run off with her. As it turned out, however, Jeff's former partner, Fisher (Steve Brodie), had followed the fugitive couple to the small mountain cabin where they were hiding out. Fisher demanded a large share of the $40,000 to keep silent, after which Kathie had brutally gunned him down. Following this, Kathie insisted that Jeff dispose of the corpse, and, after carrying out the gruesome task, he had returned to the cabin to find Kathie gone. Realizing that he, like Whit, had been completely taken in by the beautiful vixen, Jeff decided to turn his back on it all and seek the obscurity of small-town life.

The scene then shifts back to the present, as Jeff arrives at Whit's beautiful chalet. Once inside, Jeff finds that Kathie has somehow gotten back into the gangster's good graces and is now living in the plush hideaway. Whit tells Jeff that he is willing to forget the past if Jeff agrees to carry out one last job—to secure incriminating documents that will save Whit from being prosecuted for income tax evasion. Wanting to wipe the slate clean, Jeff complies, but there are deadly complications and Jeff, Whit and Kathie meet violent deaths.

The rather downbeat ending of *Out of the Past,* in which the screenwriters allowed the likable, basically good Jeff to be killed along with the real villains of the story—Whit and Kathie—was further evidence that the Hollywood gangster picture had, indeed, grown up and become more realistic. Had the picture been made several years earlier, there is no doubt that Jeff would have been allowed to redeem himself and go on to live a better life.

Rhonda Fleming and Robert Mitchum

KISS OF DEATH

A 20TH CENTURY-FOX PICTURE.   1947

Victor Mature and Richard Widmark

Howard Smith and Victor Mature

CREDITS

Directed by Henry Hathaway. *Produced by* Fred Kohlmar. *Screenplay by* Ben Hecht and Charles Lederer. *Based on a story by* Eleazar Lipsky. *Director of photography:* Norbert Brodine. *Musical score by* David Buttolph. *Running time:* 98 minutes.

CAST

Nick Bianco: Victor Mature; *Tommy Udo:* Richard Widmark; *D'Angelo:* Brian Donlevy; *Nettie:* Colleen Gray; *Ear Howser:* Taylor Holmes; *Warden:* Howard Smith; *Judge:* Robert Keith; *Sergeant William Cullen:* Karl Malden; *Williams:* Anthony Ross; *Ma Rizzo:* Mildred Dunnock; *Blondie:* Temple Texas; *Skeets:* J. Scott Smart.

Kiss of Death, one of the classic gangster-suspense films of the forties, was a landmark movie in several respects. It was the picture that introduced Richard Widmark to movie audiences, and his frightening portrayal of the psychopathic hood Tommy Udo won him instant stardom and an Academy Award nomination for best supporting actor of the year. The picture also provided Victor Mature, hitherto known primarily for his work in rather lightweight entertainments, with the challenging and emotionally draining role of Nick Bianco, the small-time criminal who tries to go

Temple Texas and Victor Mature

straight. Mature, who had proven himself a fine actor with his excellent interpretation of Doc Holliday in John Ford's *My Darling Clementine* (1940), turned in perhaps the best performance of his career in *Kiss of Death*. It was a splendid piece of screen acting by any standard, as Mature captured the many moods of a man torn between misplaced loyalty toward his criminal associates and a desire to make a clean break from his past life.

Most importantly, however, *Kiss of Death* was the first of the great gangster films to actually be shot on location, as director Henry Hathaway, fully aware that the harsh realism of the Ben Hecht–Charles Lederer script would never play on a Hollywood sound stage, refused to make *Kiss of Death* on studio sets and insisted on moving the cast and crew to New York City, where the entire production was filmed. The glittery, sumptuous "fantasy" New York, created with loving care by the Warner Brothers art department and used in nearly all the studio's gangster films, may have been more glamorous, but it would have hardly suited a downbeat crime drama like *Kiss of Death*. Hathaway's brilliant use of some gritty New York locations gave the picture a realistic tone seldom seen in films before, and it proved so effective that

Brian Donlevy, Karl Malden, Millard Mitchell, Victor Mature

Millard Mitchell, Victor Mature, Brian Donlevy

Victor Mature

it began a trend away from manufactured backgrounds and toward the use of actual settings.

Kiss of Death is also important in that it introduced a completely new kind of gangster-villain to the screen. Widmark's Tommy Udo was a far more terrifying character than any created by Robinson, Cagney, Bogart, Garfield or Ladd, and was a sadistic, inhuman "street psycho" who takes a horrible sort of glee in acts of torture and murder (evidenced by the scene in which Widmark pushes a crippled old woman, wheelchair and all, down a long flight of stairs). Though this kind of demented criminal was considerably less "appealing" than the gangsters of the past, the late forties and beyond saw an increasing number of them in

films, and even James Cagney's return to the genre in *White Heat* saw the veteran actor portraying a crazed killer.

SYNOPSIS

New York City. The drama begins on Christmas Eve, when Nick Bianco (Victor Mature), an unemployed workman wanting desperately to provide gifts for his wife and children, robs a jewelry store with the help of several thugs he has fallen in with. Several days after the robbery, Nick is captured by police and given a stiff twenty-year sentence for the offense. However, the compassionate district attorney, Louie D'Angelo (Brian

Donlevy), senses that Bianco is basically a decent man forced into crime by circumstances beyond his control. D'Angelo requests a meeting with Bianco, during which he offers to reduce the sentence if Nick agrees to inform on his accomplices. At first, Bianco refuses to turn "squealer," but later relents when his wife commits suicide and his daughters are placed in an orphanage.

Realizing that informing will give him the chance to rebuild his life, Bianco makes a deal with D'Angelo, giving the D.A. the lowdown on all his criminal contacts, for which he is let out on probation. Over the next few months, Nick marries again and secures a well-paying construction job that enables him to get his kids back. He lives a joyous, contented life for a time, but his idyll is soon threatened by Tommy Udo (Widmark), one of Nick's old mates and a vicious

psychotic who murders for kicks. As it turns out, Udo was acquitted after Nick blew the whistle on him, due to lack of evidence, and the murderous hood now wants to take revenge on Nick and his family. Realizing he will never have peace of mind until he helps the cops nail Udo, Bianco offers to set a daring trap in which he will act as bait so that Udo can be lured into attempted murder. The plan works and Udo is arrested for trying to kill Bianco but Nick is shot several times in the process. Happily, Nick recovers and returns home, finally free of his unsavory past.

Though Mature and Widmark completely dominated the film, *Kiss of Death* also featured a solid portrayal by Brian Donlevy, appearing as the soft-hearted D.A. who gives Mature a chance to redeem himself.

Victor Mature

Victor Mature

I WALK ALONE

A PARAMOUNT PICTURE. 1947

Burt Lancaster and Wendell Corey

CREDITS

A Hall B. Wallis Production. Directed by Byron Haskins. *Produced by* Hal B. Wallis. *Screenplay by* Charles Schnee. *Director of photography:* Leo Tover. *Art direction by* Hans Dreier and Franz Bachelin. *Film editor:* Arthur Schmidt. *Musical score by* Victor Young. *Running time:* 98 minutes.

CAST

Frankie Madison: Burt Lancaster; *Kay Lawrence:* Lizabeth Scott; *Noll Turner:* Kirk Douglas; *Dave:* Wendell Corey; *Mrs. Richardson:* Kristine Miller; *Maurice:* George Rigaud; *Nick Palestro:* Marc Lawrence; *Dan:* Mike Mazurki; *Skinner:* Mickey Knox; *Felix:* Roger Neury.

Hal B. Wallis, one of Hollywood's most prolific producers, had served in that capacity on several of the classic Warners gangster films, and in 1947 he returned to the genre with a moody crime melodrama entitled *I Walk Alone*. The film starred two young movie actors who were fast rising to superstardom, Burt Lancaster and Kirk Douglas, and it was produced with all the style and gloss that Paramount Pictures could muster. Douglas and Lancaster made an exceptional screen team, and the actors played against each other beautifully.

Mike Mazurki and Burt Lancaster

Burt Lancaster and Wendell Corey

Both men possessed forceful, intense styles of acting that would eventually become their trademarks, and each had a truly impressive presence on screen. The actors got along splendidly throughout the filming, becoming close and lasting friends, and *I Walk Alone* turned out to be merely the first of several films in which they appeared together over the years. Interestingly, their roles in *I Walk Alone* were somewhat similar to those they had played in two earlier gangster films, with Douglas portraying an elegantly corrupt racketeer very much like Whit Sterling in *Out of the Past,* and Lancaster appearing as an accomplice to a crime who ends up being the fall guy, not unlike his classic Swede in *The Killers.* Their co-star in *I Walk Alone* was the sultry Lizabeth Scott, whose husky-voiced delivery resembled Lauren Bacall's and who perfectly suited the role of the sexy torch singer who serves as Douglas's moll.

A tough, grim picture containing none of the warmth and humor that usually marked Wallis's crime films for Warners, *I Walk Alone* had a stark, gloomy look to it, thanks to Leo Tover's understated black-and-white photography and the decidedly downbeat musical score composed for the film by Victor Young. *I Walk Alone* also dif-

Kirk Douglas, Burt Lancaster, Lizabeth Scott

Publicity Shot with Burt Lancaster, producer Hal Wallis, Kirk Douglas

fered from the Warner Brothers pictures in that the characters were a rather unsavory lot, and even Lancaster's duped fall guy came off as rather cold-hearted, ruthless and greedy. Despite the fine acting of Lancaster and Scott, Douglas ended up stealing the show with his portrayal of Noll Turner, the flashy villain of the piece. Douglas perfectly captured the slick malevolence of the dapper gangster whose outward cool masks a strong streak of sadism. The film's rather oppressive atmosphere was greatly aided by the casting of Mike Mazurki as a murderous, giant-sized thug who does all of Douglas's dirty work.

SYNOPSIS

Frankie Madison (Lancaster) and Noll Turner (Douglas) run a profitable rum-running operation

Lizabeth Scott and Burt Lancaster

Burt Lancaster and Lizabeth Scott

during prohibition. When Madison is arrested, Turner instructs him to take the rap without involving Noll, which will leave Turner free to invest their stolen loot. Madison draws a stiff sentence, spending the next fourteen years in prison, while Turner builds a powerful empire of crime on the outside. Madison is finally released from jail and goes to see Turner, fully expecting to be cut in on the action. As it happens, however, Turner has no intention of giving Frankie anything, and gives his ex-partner the runaround when Frankie shows up at Turner's posh nightclub. Turner's accountant, Dave (Wendell Corey), explains to Madison the enormous complexities of Noll's "corporation," and informs Frankie that he has no legal right to any of it.

Unable to accept this, Frankie tries to strongarm his way into the operation, and he is worked over by Turner's chief torpedo, Dan (Mazurki). Meanwhile, Kay Lawrence (Scott), the singer at Noll's club who is also the gangster's mistress, falls in love with Frankie and offers to help him defeat Turner. She manages to enlist the aid of Dave, who is also opposed to the criminal's ruthless dealings with people and is sympathetic to Frankie's plight. Dave has enough on Turner to lock him away forever, and Turner, when he hears of the treachery brewing in his organization, has Dave killed and attempts to frame Frankie for the crime. However, the gangster's plan backfires and he is brought to justice, leaving Frankie and Kay to start a new life together.

I Walk Alone proved to be a solid boost to the careers of both Lancaster and Douglas, and the two again teamed with producer Wallis a decade later for the memorable *Gunfight at the O. K. Corral.*

169

KEY LARGO

A WARNER BROTHERS PICTURE.   1948

William Haade, Lionel Barrymore, Humphrey Bogart, Harry Lewis, Thomas Gomez, Dan Seymour, Lauren Bacall

CREDITS

Directed by John Huston *Produced by* Jerry Wald. *Screenplay by* Richard Brooks and John Huston. *Based on the play by* Maxwell Anderson. *Director of photography:* Karl Freund. *Music by* Max Steiner. *Film editor:* Rudi Fehr. *Assistant director:* Art Lueker. *Art direction:* Leo K. Kuter. *Wardrobe by* Leah Rhodes. *Make-up by* Perc Westmore. *Sound recording by* Dolph Thomas. *Running time:* 101 minutes.

CAST

Frank McCloud: Humphrey Bogart; *Nora Temple:* Lauren Bacall; *Johnny Rocco:* Edward G. Robin-

Edward G. Robinson, Claire Trevor, Lionel Barrymore,
Thomas Gomez, Humphrey Bogart, Lauren Bacall,
Harry Lewis

WARNER BROS.' **KEY LARGO**

Humphrey Bogart and Lauren Bacall

son; James Temple: Lionel Barrymore; *Gaye Dawn:* Claire Trevor; *Curley Hoff:* Thomas Gomez; *Toots:* Harry Lewis; *Angel:* Dan Seymour; *Ziggy:* Marc Lawrence.

The team of Humphrey Bogart and Lauren Bacall always meant magic on the screen, and the stars generated a sexy, electrical chemistry that never failed to enthrall audiences. They were, perhaps, the most compelling star duo of Hollywood's "Golden Age," and the four films they made together—*To Have and Have Not* (1945), *The Big Sleep* (1946), *Dark Passage* (1948) and *Key Largo* (1948)—were all solid hits with the movie-going public. The last of these—*Key Largo*—was based on a play by Maxwell Anderson, and it featured Bogart in the kind of role he had become famous

for during the forties—that of a shattered idealist whose disillusionment with the world has made him stop fighting for causes. Bacall, of course, was again featured as Bogart's love interest and, while both stars delivered their customary splendid performances, they were somewhat overshadowed in *Key Largo* by Edward G. Robinson, whose portrayal of fugitive racketeer Johnny Rocco dominated the proceedings.

Though not really a gangster film in the purest sense, *Key Largo* rates inclusion here if only for Robinson's marvelous character study, and the fact that it was the actor's first gangster part since the early forties. Throughout most of the decade, Robinson had intentionally kept clear of the genre that had made him famous, appearing instead in a string of excellent dramas like *The Sea Wolf* (1941), *Double Indemnity* (1944), *All My Sons*

Humphrey Bogart, Claire Trevor, Lauren Bacall

(1948) and *House of Strangers* (1949). In all of these, Robinson proved himself one of the truly great movie actors of the era, dazzling audiences and critics with his versatility and forever squelching the notion that gangster roles were his one and only forte. Robinson would have no doubt preferred, by the late forties, to leave the images of Little Caesar, Brother Orchid and the like far behind him, but, as it turned out, the part of Rocco in *Key Largo* was simply too good to pass up, and it gave Robinson the greatest gangster characterization of his career.

Robinson's virtuoso acting of the crude, malicious crime czar was aided considerably by the direction of John Huston, and the unforgettable opening shot of Rocco reclining, cigar in mouth, in a luxurious bubble bath, and the scene in which Robinson leans over to whisper obscenities to Lauren Bacall, have become part of gangster movie folklore. Despite Robinson's excellence, however, the actor was completely passed over in the Academy Awards race, not even receiving so much as a nomination. *Key Largo* did, however, net a Best Supporting Actress Oscar for Claire Trevor, appearing as Robinson's boozy mistress, Gae Dawn.

Humphrey Bogart, Claire Trevor, Lauren Bacall

Humphrey Bogart, Harry Lewis, Dan Seymour, Edward G. Robinson, Thomas Gomez

SYNOPSIS

Bogart played ex-army major Frank McLeod who, following distinguished war service, arrives in Key Largo, an island off the Florida coast, to visit the father and sister of a fallen army comrade, who suffered a valiant death in battle. Mr. Temple (Lionel Barrymore) and his daughter Nora (Bacall) run a small hotel on the key and, when Frank arrives, he immediately befriends the two, and gradually finds himself falling in love with Nora. The only other guests at the hotel are the mysterious "Mr. Brown," who never leaves his room, and his business associates, a group of rough-looking gentlemen who congregate in the bar almost daily.

Having stayed hidden for several days, "Mr. Brown" finally emerges, and McLeod recognizes him as crime boss Johnny Rocco (Robinson). Faced with both prosecution and deportation for his past crimes, Rocco is hiding out at the hotel until he can secure a small boat that will take him to Cuba. A one-time idealist who has been bitterly disillusioned by the war, Frank at first regards Rocco with indifference, but soon he becomes disgusted with the cocky racketeer and finds himself engaging in heated verbal exchanges with him. At one point, Frank reveals to the criminal

that he once believed it was possible for there to exist "a world where there's no place for Johnny Roccos." Later, a violent storm begins ravaging the island, and Rocco's bravado fades as the thunder and lightning intensify, making the gangster feel helpless and small ("point your gun at the storm and tell it to stop," McLeod suggests sarcastically).

Rocco vents his terror by playing a cruel joke on his alcoholic mistress, Gaye Dawn (Trevor), promising her a drink if she agrees to sing his favorite song, "Moanin' Low." However, her sodden, off-key rendition proves to be an embarrassment, and Rocco refuses her the drink. In open defiance of the gangster, McLeod walks over to the bar, pours a generous scotch and hands it to her. Later, McLeod, an experienced navigator, agrees to pilot the boat that will take Rocco and his gang to Cuba. Before they all leave, however, Gaye slips McLeod a .45 automatic, which he hides in his coat pocket. During the trip, McLeod, realizing that an evil force like Rocco must not be allowed to exist, eliminates all the gangster's henchmen, then engages Rocco in a gun battle, during which the gangster is killed.

Not surprisingly, the dramatic shootout between Bogart and Robinson at the end of *Key Largo* reminded many viewers of their deadly showdowns in the earlier gangster hits, *Bullets or Ballots* and *Kid Galahad*.

WHITE HEAT

A WARNER BROTHERS PICTURE.   1949

James Cagney and Edmund O'Brien

CREDITS

Directed by Raoul Walsh. *Produced by* Louis F. Edelman. *Screenplay by* Ivan Goff and Ben Roberts. *From a story by* Virginia Kellog. *Director of photography:* Sid Hickox. *Art direction:* Fred M. Maclean. *Film editor:* Owen Marks. *Sound recording by* Leslie Hewitt. *Music score by* Max Steiner. *Costumes by* Leah Rhodes. *Make-up by* Perc Westmore. *Special effects by* Roy Davidson and H. F. Koenekamp. *Assistant director:* Russell Saunders. *Running time:* 114 minutes.

CAST

Cody Jarrett: James Cagney; *Verna Jarrett:* Virginia Mayo; *Hank Fallon:* Edmund O'Brien; *Ma Jarrett:* Margaret Wycherly; *Big Ed Sommers:* Steve Cochran; *Evans:* John Archer; *Cotton:* Wally Cassell; *The Trader:* Fred Clarke; *Reader:* G. Pat Collins; *Happy Taylor:* Fred Coby; *Zuckie:* Ford Rainey; *Tommy Ryley:* Robert Osterloh; *Bo Creel:* Ian MacDonald; *Police Chief:* Marshall Bradford; *Ernie Trent:* Ray Montgomery; *Willie Rolf:* Milton Parsons.

White Heat is James Cagney's gangster masterpiece, a high-intensity powerhouse of a picture featuring the actor in one of his greatest performances. Having vowed never to venture into the gangster genre again after the completion of *Each*

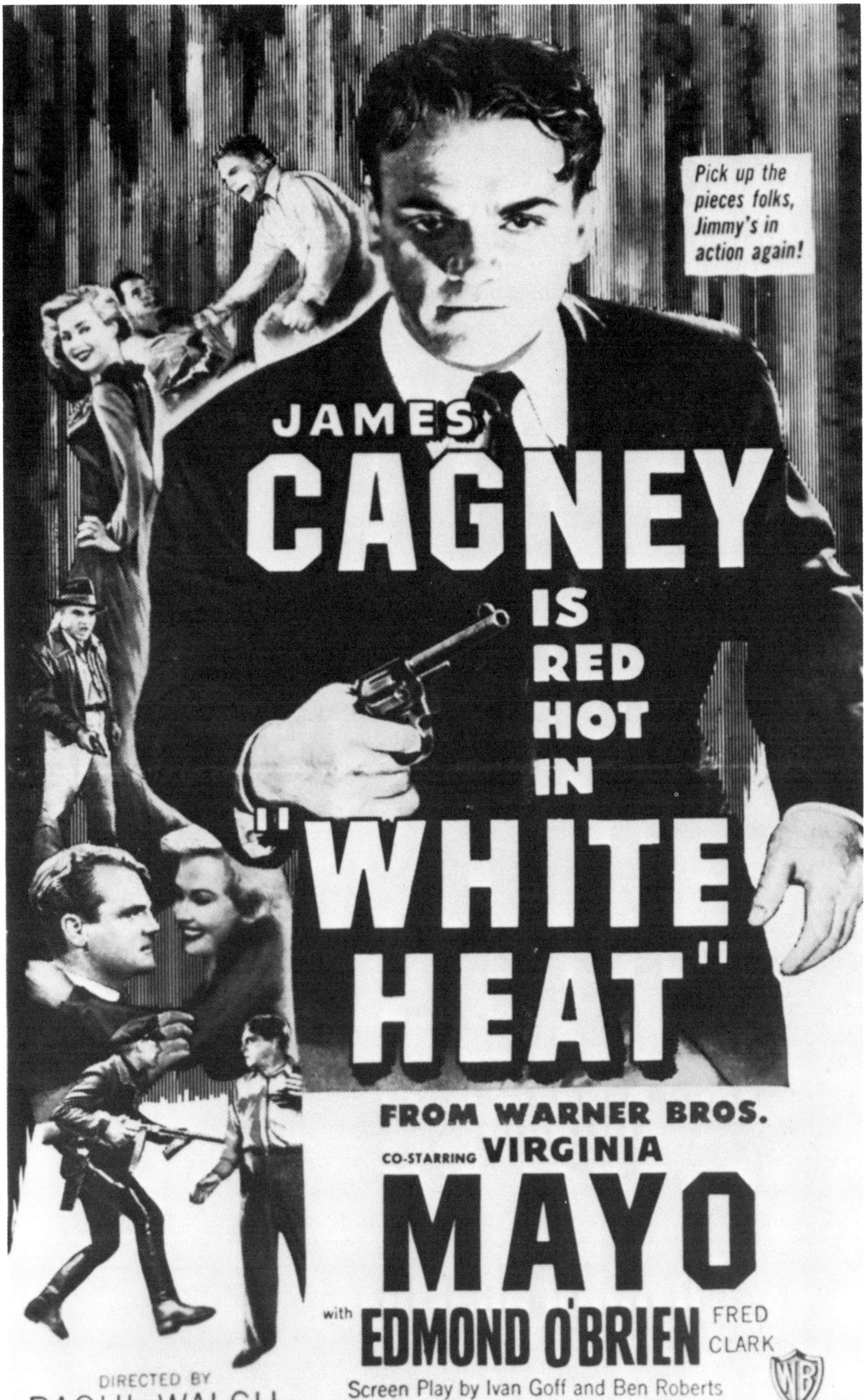
Pick up the pieces folks, Jimmy's in action again!
JAMES
CAGNEY
IS
RED
HOT
IN
"WHITE HEAT"
FROM WARNER BROS.
CO-STARRING VIRGINIA
MAYO
with
EDMOND O'BRIEN
FRED CLARK
DIRECTED BY
RAOUL WALSH
Screen Play by Ivan Goff and Ben Roberts
Suggested by a Story by Virginia Kellogg • Music by Max Steiner

Dawn I Die (1940), Cagney had spent most of the forties trying to smash his well-known tough guy image. When Cagney's contract with Warner Brothers expired in 1942, the actor "freelanced" for six years, and intentionally chose only vehicles in which he would portray soft-hearted, compassionate characters. In an effort to forever bury the memory of Tom Powers, Rocky Sullivan and the rest of his classic badmen, Cagney appeared in a string of pictures playing characters who were, literally, almost too good to be true. The films were *Johnny Come Lately* (1943), *Blood on the Sun* (1945), *Thirteen Rue Madeleine* (1946) and *The Time of Your Life* (1948), all of which were solid, well-produced showcases for the actor, but the

critical and box office response to each was considerably below that of Cagney's earlier pictures. It soon became obvious that, despite his well-intentioned efforts to escape his gangster image, audiences in general preferred the Cagney tough guy to the Cagney nice guy.

Finally, in 1949, Cagney returned to his old form in the most violent, graphic and enjoyable of the classic gangster pictures, *White Heat*. Scripted by Ivan Goff and Ben Roberts, the film cast Cagney in the legendary role of Cody Jarrett, the mother-obsessed psycho-gangster who made most of Cagney's earlier bad guys seem well behaved by comparison. Cagney gave the challenging and often outrageous part everything he had, and the famous scenes of Cody going berserk in a prison mess hall and being held at bay atop a gigantic gasoline tank, are among the best known in any gangster film.

Virginia Mayo was also excellent as Jarrett's

James Cagney and Virginia Mayo

James Cagney and Virginia Mayo

sluttish wife Verna, and Steve Cochran had the best role of his career as the slick "macho thug" Big Ed Sommers, who tries to take over the leadership of Jarrett's gang and finds himself in extra hot water. Also superb was Margaret Wycherly as Ma Jarrett, the frail yet deadly old woman who is the driving force behind Cody's criminal career.

SYNOPSIS

Cody Jarrett (Cagney), a notorious criminal with a mother fixation, commits, with the help of his gang, a train robbery, during which he is forced to kill the engineer in cold blood. Though the Treasury men investigating the crime have no evidence against him, they are certain that Jarrett is

guilty, and they assign an undercover agent, Hank Fallon (Edmund O'Brien), to try and obtain the evidence needed to put Jarrett away. When Jarrett is arrested for a lesser offense, Fallon becomes his cellmate, eventually befriending the criminal and learning all the inner workings of his gang.

Meanwhile, on the outside, Cody's rival, "Big Ed" Sommers (Cochran), seduces Jarrett's wife Verna (Mayo) and takes over as leader of the gang. When this happens, Ma Jarrett (Wycherly) visits Cody in prison, telling him what Ed has done and vowing to take care of the treacherous thug herself. Despite Cody's pleas that she stay away from the formidable Sommers, Ma Jarrett later has a showdown with the gangster, during which the old woman is killed. During the prison mess hour the following week, Cody is told of her death and

181

goes violently berserk; prison officials are forced to put him in a straitjacket. When he finally recovers from the shock, Cody engineers an ingenious escape plan with Fallon and several other inmates, and they manage to flee from custody.

Returning home with Fallon, Cody brutally guns down Big Ed, then roughs Verna up to teach her a lesson. With Ed out of the way, Cody resumes the leadership of his gang, and plans the daring robbery of a chemical plant as their next job. Now regarding Fallon as his right-hand man, Cody tells him the mechanics of the elaborate heist, after which Fallon relays the information to the T-men. On the day of the robbery, the T-men surround the chemical plant, and wait to ambush Jarrett. One by one, the members of Cody's gang are killed off, and Jarrett meets his own death atop a high gasoline tank.

The final scene of *White Heat*, in which Cody is enveloped by blazing chemical explosions after being shot several times with a high-powered rifle, was, without question, the most spectacular death ever afforded a screen gangster.

Edmund O'Brien and James Cagney

James Cagney

KISS TOMORROW GOODBYE

A WARNER BROTHERS PICTURE.   1950

James Cagney (1)

CREDITS

A William Cagney Production. Directed by Gordon Douglas. *Produced by* William Cagney. *Screenplay by* Harry Brown. *Based on the novel by* Horace McCoy. *Director of photography:* Peverell Marley. *Art direction:* Wiard Ihnen. *Set decorations:* Joe Kish. *Sound recording by* William Lynch. *Film editors:* Truman K. Wood and Walter Hannemann. *Musical score:* Carmen Dragon. *Make-up by* Otis Malcolm. *Special effects by* Paul Eagler. *Running time:* 102 minutes.

CAST

Ralph Cotter: James Cagney; *Holiday:* Barbara Payton; *Inspector Weber:* Ward Bond; *Mandon:* Luther Adler; *Margaret Dobson:* Helena Carter; *Jinx:* Steve Brodie; *Vic Mason:* Rhys Williams; *Reece:* Barton MacLane; *Ezra Dobson:* Herbert Hayes; *Doc Green:* Frank Reicher; *Tolgate:* John Litel; *District Attorney:* Dan Riss; *Cobbett:* John Halloran; *Byers:* William Frawley; *Detective Fowler:* Kenneth Tobey; *Carleton:* Neville Brand; *Ralph's Brother:* William Cagney.

The success of *White Heat* prompted Warners to produce a similar film the following year, in which James Cagney would again be featured as a psychopathic hoodlum. This time, the production would be shot by Warners in association with

184

Luther Adler and James Cagney

James Cagney and Barbara Payton

William Cagney Productions, the company founded by the actor's brother in 1943. The William Cagney Company was a modest, well-run family operation (James served as vice-president) that had produced three of the actor's vehicles—*Johnny Come Lately, Blood on the Sun* and *The Time of Your Life*—of the mid-forties. *Kiss Tomorrow Goodbye*, released in 1950, marked the company's first foray into the gangster genre, and it emerged as a gritty, dark-spirited little melo-

drama, in which Cagney portrayed one of his most unappealing characters.

Though certainly not the equal of *White Heat* in any respect, *Kiss Tomorrow Goodbye* had plenty going for it in all departments, and remains one of the actor's most underrated crime pictures. Upon its release, most critics dismissed it as an obvious attempt to capitalize on Cagney's sensational Cody Jarrett, which, in a way, it was. But it is indeed a shame that Warners chose to make *Kiss Tomorrow*

Goodbye so similar to *White Heat* and thus invite comparison, for, taken on its own merits, it is a most enjoyable genre film.

Cagney appeared as a kind of middle-aged Tom Powers, a vicious, ruthless thug whose penchant for cold-blooded murder is matched only by his barbaric treatment of women. The grapefruit treatment which Mae Clarke received in *The Public Enemy* was a light pleasantry compared to Cagney's abuse of Barbara Payton in this film. In one of the climactic scenes, he slaps her repeatedly with a rolled-up towel, which certainly ranks as the most brutal of Cagney's screen assaults on a mistress. *Kiss Tomorrow Goodbye* was also similar to *The Public Enemy* in its physical production; the settings and the costumes were especially reminiscent of the thirties classic, as was the cinematography of the veteran Peverell Marley. Much of the picture had a dark, murky look, and many scenes were photographed in an especially harsh shade of black-and-white, giving *Kiss Tomorrow Goodbye* a stark ugliness not unlike an episode of the "Highway Patrol" television series of the fifties. Barbara Payton, the blond actress who had a brief fling at stardom, appeared as Cagney's troublesome girlfriend, a role obviously modelled after Virginia Mayo's part in *White Heat*, but without the humorous touches.

SYNOPSIS

Ralph Cotter (Cagney), a violent, homicidal gangster, escapes from prison with the help of his pal Jinx (Steve Brodie) and the lovely Holiday (Payton), the sister of one of Cotter's "boys" who had been killed in a robbery several years before. Hiding out in town, Cotter eludes detection by changing his name and hiring a brilliant but larcenous attorney (Luther Adler) to advise him. The lawyer pulls certain strings at City Hall and gets Cotter a gun permit, which allows the crimi-nal to legally carry his prized automatic at all times.

Cotter reorganizes his old gang and pulls off a series of successful robberies in the city. Later, however, he is visited by two crooked cops, Inspector Weber (Ward Bond) and Officer Reese (Barton MacLane), who attempt to shake Cotter down. Through the efforts of Holiday, Jinx and his attorney, however, the gangster obtains damning evidence against Weber and Reese. Threatening to turn it over to the district attorney, Cotter soon has the dishonest officers dancing to *his* tune. Later, Holiday becomes Ralph's mistress and she threatens to kill the gangster if he is ever unfaithful to her. Not taking the threat seriously, Cotter charms a wealthy heiress, Margaret Dobson (Helena Carter) into marriage, and manages to endear himself to her powerful, influential father, Ezra Dobson (Herbert Hayes).

Completely oblivious to Cotter's criminal background, Dobson offers Ralph a high-paying executive position with one of his companies. Deciding to turn his back on crime and accept his father-in-law's offer, Ralph returns to his old apartment to pick up his belongings, unaware that Holiday has found out about his marriage. When she tells him that she knows all about his plans to leave her and go straight, Cotter tries to convince Holiday that he has only been stringing Margaret along, and that he intends to divorce her and cut Holiday in on the settlement. Holiday refuses to believe this, however, and kills Cotter with her brother's revolver.

Kiss Tomorrow Goodbye has the distinction of being the only classic gangster film to actually be banned in certain circles for its excessive violence. Apparently shocked by the overall viciousness of Cagney's character, Ohio forbad the picture from being shown anywhere in the state, referring to it as a "sadistic presentation of brutality."

THE ASPHALT JUNGLE

A METRO-GOLDWYN-MAYER PICTURE.   1950

Louis Calhern and Marilyn Monroe

Marc Lawrence and Sam Jaffe

CREDITS

Directed by John Huston. *Produced by* Arthur Hornblow, Jr. *Screenplay by* Ben Maddow and John Huston. *From the novel by* W. R. Burnett. *Director of photography:* Harold Rossen. *Musical score by* Miklos Rozsa. *Film editor:* George Boemler. *Art direction:* Cedric Gibbons. *Running time:* 112 minutes.

CAST

Dix Handley: Sterling Hayden; *Alonzo D. Emmerich:* Louis Calhern; *Doll Conovan:* Jean Hagen; *Riedenschneider:* Sam Jaffe; *Gus Minissi:* James Whitmore; *Cobby:* Marc Lawrence; *Hardy:* John McIntire; *Louis Ciavelli:* Anthony Caruso; *Maria Ciavelli:* Teresa Celli; *Angela Phinlay:* Marilyn Monroe; *Dietrich:* Barry Kelley; *Timmons:* William Davis; *May Emmerich:* Dorothy Tree; *Bob Brannen:* Brad Dexter; *Swanson:* John Maxwell.

The Asphalt Jungle, one of the most acclaimed gangster movies of the fifties, was directed by John Huston and featured first-rate performers such as Sterling Hayden, Louis Calhern, Sam Jaffe, Jean Hagen, James Whitmore and the then-unknown Marilyn Monroe in some of the finest acting of their careers. The film, which dealt with a group of small-time criminals who engineer a million-dollar jewelry heist, was a solid success at the box office and garnered excellent notices from the critics, many of whom felt that Huston, with his brilliant direction and the meticulous way he explored each of the characters, had brought the gangster film to new heights. Interestingly, however, despite all the praise heaped upon the picture and the people who made it, *The Asphalt Jungle* came about almost by accident, and was actually the result of another film project's failure to materialize.

Huston, fresh from such triumphs as *The Treasure of the Sierra Madre* and *Key Largo*, had signed a lucrative contract with MGM in 1950, and his first assignment for the studio was to have been the direction of a multi-million-dollar extravaganza about ancient Rome, *Quo Vadis*, which would feature an all-star cast headed by Gregory

Peck, Elizabeth Taylor and Huston's actor-father, Walter. While the cast and crew were scouting locations in Rome, however, Gregory Peck was stricken with a painful eye infection that put him out of commission, forcing the studio to put *Quo Vadis* on hold and to come up with another project on which Huston could work in the meantime. Familiar with Huston's winning track record, MGM gave him virtually a free hand to select any vehicle he wanted, and the one he chose was *The Asphalt Jungle*, a best-selling crime novel by W. R. Burnett. Huston reportedly displayed more enthusiasm for the new venture than he had toward *Quo Vadis*, which isn't surprising, since the rough-

hewn story of gangsters and betrayal was probably more his cup of tea than the overblown epic of ancient times. (Huston, in fact, never returned to the *Quo Vadis* enterprise, and it was eventually made the following year with a different cast under the direction of Mervyn LeRoy.)

Huston's affinity for the material shows through in every scene of *The Asphalt Jungle,* and while the film contained a clinical realism similar to *Kiss of Death, Out of the Fog* and other crime dramas of the late forties, it also exhibited virtuoso lighting and camera work that made it highly reminiscent of the Warners classics, and Huston's superb use of shadows and camera angles to heighten the atmosphere of certain scenes cannot help but remind the viewer of the look of pictures like *Angels With Dirty Faces* and *The Roaring Twenties*.

SYNOPSIS

Doc Riedenschneider (Sam Jaffe), an aging criminal mastermind, is released after serving a long prison term. Realizing that he is in the twilight of his years, it is Doc's all-consuming ambition to pull off one last spectacular job on which to retire, and he begins planning the robbery of a high-class jewelry exchange, the profits from which will exceed a million dollars. Now destitute after his stretch in the big house, Doc realizes he will need financial backing to see the caper through, and he manages to obtain it from a well-to-do bookie friend named Cobby (Marc Lawrence). Later, Emmerich (Louis Calhern), a prominent but shady attorney with contacts in the criminal underworld, learns of the impending heist and asks to see Doc, offering to buy all the stolen jewelry for a handsome price. As it turns out, however, Emmerich is actually deeply in debt and in desperate need of money, and he intends to double-cross Doc by running off with the jewels and selling them himself.

Some time before the robbery is scheduled to take place, Doc assembles a gang of experienced burglars and instructs them as to how the job will be carried out. The small band of thieves includes Dix (Sterling Hayden), a young man utterly disillusioned and alienated from the world, who desperately yearns to recapture the beauty of his childhood in Kentucky, and who hopes that his "take" from the robbery will allow him to return there; Gus (James Whitmore), the getaway driver; and Louis (Anthony Caruso), a master safecracker.

The ensuing robbery is a complete success until the final moments, when Louis is accidentally killed when one of the guns goes off in his direction. Later on, when Emmerich is shown the lucrative haul by Doc and Dix, the lawyer attempts to steal it with the help of his strongarm henchman Bannerman (Brad Dexter). Before they are

Louis Calhern, Sterling Hayden, Jean Hagen, Sam Jaffe

191

able to get away, however, Dix kills Bannerman but is himself wounded in the exchange. Faced with the threat of scandal and ruination because of what has happened, Emmerich commits suicide. Doc is later apprehended by the police, and Dix, despite his injuries, manages to somehow make it back to Kentucky, dying just as he reaches his childhood home.

Huston's exceptional handling of the material won him Oscar nominations for his direction and screenplay. Marilyn Monroe, who appeared in *The Asphalt Jungle* briefly as Emmerich's mistress, was hired by Joseph L. Mankiewicz the same year to do a similar stint in his blockbuster *All About Eve*.

Sterling Hayden, Brad Dexter, Louis Calhern, Sam Jaffe

THE ENFORCER

A UNITED STATES PICTURE FOR WARNER BROTHERS.   1951

Roy Roberts and Ted De Corsia

CREDITS

Directed by Bretaigne Windust. *Produced by* Milton Sperling. *Screenplay by* Martin Rackin. *Director of photography:* Robert Burkes. *Music by* David Buttolph. *Film editor:* Fred Allen. *Assistant director:* Chuck Hansen. *Art director:* Charles H. Clarke. *Set decorations by* William Kuehl. *Sound recording by* Dolph Thomas. *Running time:* 87 minutes.

CAST

Martin Ferguson: Humphrey Bogart; *Albert Mendoza:* Everett Sloane; *Big Babe Lazich:* Zero

Roy Roberts, Zero Mostel,
Humphrey Bogart

Humphrey Bogart and Ted De Corsia

Mostel; *Joseph Rico:* Ted De Corsia; *Captain Nelson:* Roy Roberts; *Duke Malloy:* Lawrence Tolan; *Herman:* Bob Steele; *Sgt. Whitlow:* King Donovan; *Zaca:* Jack Lambert; *Vince:* John Kellog.

By 1950, Humphrey Bogart had become one of the world's most popular and celebrated stars with a string of truly stunning film performances behind him. The forties had been a rich and rewarding decade for the actor, and it could be argued that no other star of the period appeared in so many excellent motion pictures. Like Robinson and Cagney, Bogart had abandoned the gangster genre and moved on to more distinguished portrayals, but in 1951 he accepted Warner Brothers' offer to play the title role in *The Enforcer,* which would be his first appearance in a gangster picture since 1942.

The film was a clinical, no-holds-barred drama dealing with an infamous organization known as Murder, Inc., a group of cold-blooded professional killers who will do anyone in for the right price. These were a far cry from the traditional gangsters of old, who, for the most part, limited their victims to the members of rival gangs, but were a new and infinitely more dangerous breed of criminal, whose business it was to murder strangers that someone simply wanted out of the way. Bogart, on the side of law and order in his return to the genre, played a crusading district attorney who, almost single-handedly, unravels the mystery of Murder, Inc. and smashes it.

A taut, suspenseful piece of movie-making, *The Enforcer* had the look and feel of a law enforcement documentary, as the Bogart character slowly and meticulously builds his case out of a thousand tiny loose ends. Bogart was given fine support by

196

top-flight character actors like Zero Mostel, Ted De Corsia, Roy Roberts and Everett Sloane, the latter portraying one of the most frightening gangster villains in history. Sloane has seldom equalled his performance as Albert Mendoza, the small-time thug who organizes Murder, Inc., and builds it into a lucrative nationwide racket. Sloane's Mendoza was evil incarnate, a malevolent monster chilling audiences to the marrow with his offhand, casual approach to bloodshed, and the almost hypnotic control he exerts over the killers who work for him. Ted De Corsia was also splendid as Joseph Rico, Mendoza's former lieutenant who betrays him to the police, as was Zero Mostel, appearing as a nervous petty crook who joins Murder, Inc., and lives to regret it.

Even though tame by today's standards, *The Enforcer* was pretty strong stuff for the early fifties, filled with graphic death scenes (like De Corsia's fatal plunge off a high ledge at the Hall of Justice; and the gruesome discovery, in a junked auto, of the corpse of a once beautiful young woman, the victim of one of Mendoza's killers). Despite its lurid touches, however, *The Enforcer* was a high-quality crime drama, providing Bogart with several superb scenes in which he attempts to break the various mob informants by subjecting them to a merciless third degree.

SYNOPSIS

Assistant D. A. Martin Ferguson (Bogart) arrests the leader of Murder, Inc., Albert Mendoza (Sloane), and his chief assassin Joseph Rico (De Corsia). In exchange for leniency, Rico makes a deal with Ferguson to testify against Mendoza, and tells the D.A. everything he knows about his boss's "murder for hire" racket. While Rico is telling his story, however, someone takes a shot at him with a high-powered rifle from a rooftop adjacent to the Hall of Justice. Though the bullet misses him, Rico realizes that there will be other attempts on his life by Mendoza's network of killers, and he panics. Managing to temporarily distract the cops who are guarding him, Rico tries to escape out a high window and falls several stories to his death.

Determined to see his case against Mendoza through despite the loss of his star witness, Ferguson plays the tape recording of Rico's testimony, and the scene flashes back to when Rico and Mendoza first began their unholy alliance. It was in a small neighborhood restaurant several years earlier, where Mendoza had met Rico and revealed his plans to start a "murder for hire" business. He confessed to Rico that, indeed, he was at the café that evening to carry out his first

197

contract killing, as a client had paid him a hefty sum to murder the owner. Mendoza then calmly slit the man's throat, but, at just that instant, Tony Vetto and his little girl Angela happened to walk into the café. Rico had told Ferguson how the child looked at Mendoza with her "big blue eyes," and how she had screamed after witnessing the murder. Rico then related that, years later, Mendoza had ordered his assassins to eliminate Tony and Angela and, during this part of the testimony, Ferguson remembered that the cops later discovered the murdered girl's body in an abandoned auto on the outskirts of town.

Suddenly, Ferguson switches off the tape and, realizing that something Rico said might be the clue that cracks the case, he unearths the autopsy report on Angela, which reveals that the dead girl had *brown* eyes. Seeing this, Ferguson realizes that Mendoza's men killed the wrong girl, and that Angela Vetto, the one witness who can put Mendoza away for life, is still alive. Later, Ferguson locates her, and tells his assistant, "I want to see Mendoza's face when he looks into those 'big blue eyes' again."

Humphrey Bogart's return to the gangster genre proved a most enjoyable one, even though, this time, he was on the right side of the law. It wouldn't be very long, however, before Bogart would be back as a gun-wielding bad guy in his last, and perhaps greatest, gangster characterization—Glenn Griffin in *The Desperate Hours.*

Roy Roberts, Patricia Joiner, Humphrey Bogart

LOVE ME OR LEAVE ME

A METRO-GOLDWYN-MAYER PICTURE.   1955

James Cagney, Doris Day, Robert Keith

CREDITS

Directed by Charles Vidor. *Produced by* Joe Pasternak. *Screenplay by* Daniel Fuchs and Isobel Lennart. *Based on a story by* Daniel Fuchs. *Director of photography:* Arthur E. Arling. *Film editor:* Ralph E. Winters. *Art direction:* Cedric Gibbons and Urie McCleary. *Musical director:* George Stoll. *Sound recording by* Wesley C. Miller. *Choreographer:* Alex Romero. *Costumes by* Helen Rose. *Special effects by* Warren Newcombe. *Miss Day's music by* Percy Faith. *Running time:* 122 minutes.

CAST

Ruth Etting: Doris Day; *Martin "The Gimp" Snyder:* James Cagney; *Johnny Alderman:* Cameron Mitchell; *Bernard Loomis:* Robert Keith; *Frobisher:* Tom Tully; *Georgie:* Harry Bellaver; *Paul Hunter:* Richard Gaines; *Fred Taylor:* Peter Leeds; *Eddie Fulton:* Claude Stroud; *Greg Trent:* John Harding; *Jingle Girl:* Audrey Young; *Dancer:* Dorothy Abbott; *Orry:* Jay Adler; *Hostess:* Veda Ann Borg; *Claire:* Claire Carleton; *Stage Manager:* Benny Burt.

The 1950's were, among other things, the era of the big-screen "biopic," and Hollywood churned

Doris Day and James Cagney

out an impressive number of glossy, big-budget biographies during this period. These pictures usually dealt with the life and career of a well-known show business personality, and among the stars to receive the treatment were Lon Chaney, Benny Goodman, Glenn Miller, Eddie Foy, Joe E. Lewis, Jane Frohman, Lillian Roth, Helen Morgan and George Raft. Though usually well-received by audiences, films of this type were frequently criticized for glossing over the more candid aspects of the subject's life and not telling the story the way it *really* happened.

In 1955, MGM produced a film that was truly above such criticism, a hard-hitting, no-holds-barred biography of the famous 1920's torch singer Ruth Etting, entitled *Love Me or Leave Me* and starring Doris Day and James Cagney. Unlike most films of its kind, it apparently presented the details of the characters' lives with complete candor, including the unpleasant and sordid aspects, and, aside from a rather contrived happy ending, appeared to be a completely honest depiction of Miss Etting's obsessive relationship

Doris Day and
Cameron Mitchell

of sensual allure to her delivery of the songs while depicting the offstage Ruth as something of a virtuous innocent.

SYNOPSIS

Ruth Etting (Day), a farm girl from Nebraska, is determined to make it as a singer, and she leaves home to take the big city of Chicago by storm. Once there, however, her attempts at being discovered prove fruitless, and she manages to find employment only in the chorus line of a chintzy nightclub. When her boss, a small-time hustler, hears that she harbors dreams of becoming a singing star, he offers to give Etting a featured spot if she agrees to go home with him, but Ruth refuses and quits.

Promising herself that she will hit the big time without compromising her virtue, Ruth manages

Publicity shots of Doris Day

with real-life gangster Martin Snyder. One reason *Love Me or Leave Me* was more truthful than most fifties screen biographies was that MGM wisely secured the permission of Etting, Snyder and the other people dealt with in the story, thus allowing screenwriters Daniel Fuchs and Isobel Lennart a virtual free hand in translating the facts to the screen. The result was a superb motion picture, containing the finest performance ever given by Day and featuring Cagney in his last grand gangster tour-de-force.

Though perhaps not qualifying as a gangster film *per se*, *Love Me or Leave Me* is important to the history of the genre because it represented Cagney's final appearance in this kind of role, and his marvelous acting brought him a richly deserved Academy Award nomination. The major criticism of *Love Me or Leave Me* was that Doris Day, with her "girl next door" screen image, seemed miscast as the sexy torch singer, but a viewing of the picture makes this opinion hard to fathom. She is excellent in the role, giving just the right amount to land a singing job at another small club the following week. One night during her engagement there, she meets a local racketeer, Marty "The Gimp" Snyder (Cagney), who, impressed with her talent, offers to become her agent and business manager. Assuring her that his intentions are honorable, Snyder books her into a $2500 a week gig at a high-class nightclub, and gradually takes over her life, "Svengali" fashion. A recording contract follows, along with a string of movie deals, and Ruth at last attains the success she always dreamed of. Later, however, Snyder, convincing Ruth that she owes him something for all he has done, forces her into marriage.

Soon, the rigors of her career and marriage to a man she does not love make an emotional wreck of Ruth, who turns to alcohol as a means of escape. Later on, she falls in love with her musician friend Johnny Alderman (Cameron Mitchell) and demands that Snyder give her a divorce. Snyder shoots Alderman, who luckily escapes with only a minor injury. When Ruth walks out on Snyder, her career starts to decline and she soon realizes that the gangster was, in a strange way, an integral part of her success. Finally awakening to the unhappiness he has caused her, Snyder tries to make amends by building his own nightclub and hiring Ruth as the opening night headliner.

In addition to Cagney's Oscar nomination for Best Actor, *Love Me or Leave Me* received five other nominations as well, for best motion picture story, screenplay, sound recording, scoring of a musical film and song.

Cameron Mitchell and Doris Day

Doris Day

202

I DIED A THOUSAND TIMES

A WARNER BROTHERS PICTURE.   1955

Lee Marvin, Gonzalez Gonzalez, Earl Holliman, Jack Palance, Shelley Winters

CREDITS

Directed by Stuart Heisler. *Produced by* Willis Goldbeck. *Screenplay by* W. R. Burnett. *Director of photography:* Ted McCord. *Art direction:* Edward Carrere. *Film editor:* Clarence Kolster. *Sound by* Charles B. Lang. *Set decorator:* William L. Kuehl. *Assistant director:* Chuck Hansen. *Music by* David Buttolph. *Wardrobe by* Moss Mabry. *Make-up supervisor:* Gordon Bau. *Running time:* 109 minutes.

CAST

Roy Earle: Jack Palance; *Marie Garson:* Shelley Winters; *Velma:* Lori Nelson; *Babe:* Lee Marvin; *Red:* Earl Holliman; *Big Mack:* Lon Chaney; *Louis Mendoza:* Perry Lopez; *Doc Banton:* Howard St. John; *Pa:* Ralph Moody; *Ma:* Olive Carey; *Kranmer:* Joseph Millikin; *Lon:* Dick Davalos; *Sheriff:* Bill Kennedy; *Ed:* Dub Taylor; *Deputy:* Dick Reeves.

The practice of remaking classic movies dates back to the thirties and forties, when such immortal silents as *Dr. Jekyll and Mr. Hyde, The Phantom of the Opera, The Hunchback of Notre Dame, The Three Musketeers* and the like were redone by the major studios. Remakes continued to be a popular Hollywood commodity throughout the fifties, sixties and seventies, and there are report-

Earl Holliman, Jack Palance,
Shelley Winters

Jack Palance and Joseph Millikin

edly plans currently in the works to remake at least a half-dozen classics from the past, utilizing all the modern advances such as Dolby stereo sound and the latest special effects techniques. Though there have certainly been plenty of them, remakes, by and large, are generally disappointing to audiences and looked down on by critics, primarily because, more often than not, they fail to match the quality of the original.

There have been scores of remakes in virtually every popular film genre (especially the horror picture and the western) but, for some reason, the gangster cinema managed to produce only a few, one of the most faithful of which was Warner Brothers' 1955 production of *I Died a Thousand Times*, a large-scale color rehash of Bogart's *High Sierra*. It contained almost exactly the same characters and script as the original, with Jack Palance and Shelley Winters assuming the roles played by Bogart and Ida Lupino. Though not widely regarded at the time of its release, no doubt because it didn't even come close to *High Sierra* in terms of style and dramatic punch, *I Died a Thousand Times* does not deserve to be dismissed entirely either. It was, in all fairness, one of the lushest and most expensively mounted gangster

Shelley Winters
and Bill Kennedy

movies of the fifties, blessed with beautiful color photography and a typically powerful and brassy Warners fifties-style music score.

Also, the picture contained a striking interpretation of Roy "Mad Dog" Earle by Palance, who, while lacking Bogart's sympathetic qualities, was perhaps better able to explore the character's darker side. Palance's Roy Earle was a much more threatening figure than Bogart's, making the scenes in which he manhandles his young criminal cohorts (played by Lee Marvin and Earl Holliman in the remake) seem more believable. Aside from Palance's performance and the picture's technical excellence, *I Died a Thousand Times* is also worth noting for the brief but impressive cameo by the veteran Lon Chaney, who superbly played "Big Mack," the dying gangster chief who engineers Roy Earle's release from prison.

Though admittedly not as entertaining overall as the 1940 film, *I Died a Thousand Times* is nonetheless one of the best-produced of the gangster remakes, and is a highly enjoyable if somewhat campy and overblown example of a fifties crime drama.

Bill Kennedy and Shelley Winters

THE DESPERATE HOURS

A PARAMOUNT PICTURE.   1955

Humphrey Bogart

CREDITS

Directed and produced by William Wyler. *Associate producer:* Robert Wyler. *Screenplay by* Joseph Hayes, based on his novel and play. *Director of photography:* Lee Garmes. *Filmed in* VistaVision. *Film editor:* Robert Swink. *Assistant director:* C. C. Coleman. *Art direction by* Hal Pereira and Joseph MacMillan Johnson. *Set decorations by* Sam Comer and Grace Gregory. *Costumes by* Edith Head. *Make-up by* Wally Westmore. *Running time:* 112 minutes.

CAST

Glenn Griffin: Humphrey Bogart; *Dan Hilliard:* Fredric March; *Jesse Bard:* Arthur Kennedy; *Eleanor Hilliard:* Martha Scott; *Chuck:* Gig Young; *Hal Griffin:* Dewey Martin; *Cindy:* Mary Murphy; *Ralphie:* Richard Eyer; *Kobish:* Robert Middleton; *Detective:* Alan Reed; *Winston:* Bert Freed; *Masters:* Ray Collins; *Carson:* Whit Bissell; *Fredericks:* Ray Teal; *Detective:* Michael Moore.

Joseph Hayes's play *The Desperate Hours*, which dealt with the ordeal of a suburban family being held hostage by three escaped convicts, had a smashing Broadway debut in 1955. It featured Paul Newman, at the very start of his career and as yet a relative unknown to audiences, as the lead criminal Glenn Griffin, and it also starred Karl Malden in the emotionally taxing role of Dan Hilliard, the "solid citizen" whose family is terror-

206

ized by Griffin and his two henchmen. The play was exceptionally well acted, and the cast was able to sustain a mood of taut suspense for nearly two hours. Newman in particular delivered a powerful performance that oozed with a kind of virulant, macho menace, and it wasn't long after the play finished its lengthy run that Newman became a star.

The drama had obvious similarities to *The Petrified Forest* in that it dealt with a murderous fugitive holding a group of people at bay, only this time the gangster was practically the whole show, not merely a supporting character as Duke Mantee had been. In a way, Glenn Griffin ranks as the Macbeth of gangster roles, a long and dramatically challenging part that required the actor playing it to be on stage for most of the drama. Newman had risen to the difficult task superbly on the stage, but there was only one actor who could do the role justice in the motion picture version.

By 1955, Humphrey Bogart was at the peak of his long and distinguished career and could choose virtually any screen role he wanted. Not surprisingly, Bogart fell in love with *The Desperate Hours* and purchased the movie rights to it not long after the Broadway premiere. Initially, Bogart felt that it would make a superb vehicle for himself and his good friend Spencer Tracy, but this version never materialized, reportedly because neither

Richard Eyer and Martha Scott

actor would consent to second billing. The part of Dan Hilliard was given to Fredric March, and William Wyler, who had guided Bogart through one of his most memorable portrayals of the thirties—Baby Face Martin in *Dead End*—was hired to direct.

Released by Paramount in late 1955, *The Desperate Hours* featured exceptional, Oscar-caliber performances from Bogart and March, and it was one of the first major gangster films to get the full wide-screen treatment (it was shot in Paramount's VistaVision process). Wyler's direction was, of course, marvelous, and he gave *The Desperate Hours* the same kind of documentary-style realism that he had employed to such great effect in the earlier *Detective Story* (1951). This was achieved by photographing the drama in long, uninterrupted takes, and keeping the proceedings completely void of any background music.

SYNOPSIS

Three escaped convicts—Glenn Griffin (Bogart), his younger brother Hal (Dewey Martin) and Sam Kobish (Robert Middleton)—take temporary refuge in a quiet suburban neighborhood, invading the home of banker Dan Hilliard (March) and his family. Deciding to hide out at the Hilliard

Humphrey Bogart

207

residence until they can make a safe getaway, Griffin and his two henchmen hold the family hostage, threatening to kill them all if anyone tips off the cops. The three grubby criminals seem horribly out of place in the immaculate suburban home, and pass their days by terrorizing Hilliard, his wife Eleanor (Martha Scott), their daughter Cindy (Mary Murphy) and young son Ralphie (Richard Eyer). So that none of the family's friends or co-workers will suspect that there's anything wrong, Griffin allows the family to go about their daily routines . . . Hilliard reports to work at the bank as usual, and Cindy goes on several dates with her boyfriend Chuck (Gig Young). Though Hilliard manages to pull off a charade of normalcy, Cindy's behavior is elusive and erratic, which makes Chuck suspicious.

Meanwhile, Sheriff Jesse Bard (Arthur Kennedy) learns that the Griffin brothers and Kobish are holed up at the Hilliard's, and he places an armed surveillance team in the house next door, so that the movements of the criminals can be observed around the clock. Later, Hal is killed when he leaves his brother and Kobish to try and "make it on his own," and Kobish and Griffin are eventually forced out of the residence and gunned down by police.

The Desperate Hours was, for the most part, played against a single setting—the interior of the Hilliard home—but the pacing of the film never bogged down for an instant, thanks to Wyler's knowing direction and the constantly gliding camera of Lee Garmes.

Gig Young, Martha Scott, Richard Eyer

AL CAPONE

AN ALLIED ARTISTS PICTURE.   1959

Rod Steiger

Rod Steiger *(c)*

CREDITS

Directed by Richard Wilson. *Produced by* John H. Burrows and Leonard J. Ackerman. *Screenplay by* Marvin Wald and Henry F. Greenberg. *Director of photography:* Lucien Ballard. *Film editor:* Walter Hannemann. *Sound recording by* Tom Lambert. *Production manager:* Lonnie D'Orsa. *Production designer:* Hilyard Brown. *Assistant director:* Lindsley Parsons, Jr. *Music by* David Raksin. *Set decorations:* Joe Kish. *Dialogue supervisor:* Joe Sargent. *Special effects:* Dave Koehler. *Make-up by* Dave Grayson. *Running time:* 105 minutes.

CAST

Al Capone: Rod Steiger; *Maureen:* Fay Spain; *Schaefer:* James Gregory; *Keely:* Martin Balsam; *Johnny Torrio:* Nehemiah Persoff; *Bugs Moran:* Murvyn Vye; *Big Jim Colosimo:* Joe De Santis; *Hymie Weiss:* Lewis Charles; *O'Banion:* Robert Gist; *Bones Corelli:* Sandy Kenyon; *Mr. Brancato:* Raymond Bailey; *Tony Genaro:* Al Ruscio; *Joe Lorenzo:* Louis Quinn; *Scalisi:* Ron Soble; *Anselmo:* Steve Gravers; *Ben Hoffman:* Ben Ari.

Of the several screen biographies of real-life gangsters, 1958's *Al Capone* ranks as one of the best. Capone remains perhaps the most famous racketeer in history, and he virtually ruled all gangland activity in Chicago during the twenties. His meteoric criminal career has been explored in numerous books, all of which have had impressive sales, and there have also been several motion pictures dealing with his exploits. Though his name was not used, Capone served as the model for the characters played by Edward G. Robinson in *Little Caesar* and Paul Muni in *Scarface*, and the films dealing with Capone himself have never failed to fascinate viewers. Several fine actors have attempted to capture the essence of Capone in their portrayals of the gangster, most notably Jason Robards, Ben Gazzara and Neville Brand, but none managed to etch as memorable a portrait as Rod Steiger.

In playing the role, Steiger had several advantages that the other stars were lacking, not the least of which was a striking physical resemblance to Capone. Also, Steiger's intense, volatile style of acting perhaps better suited the public's concept of what the real Capone was probably like, and was thus far more believable than the surprisingly subtle interpretations of the other actors. The film

Fay Spain and Rod Steiger

Fay Spain and Rod Steiger

was produced by Allied Artists, one of the most prolific and successful "B" picture factories of the 1950's, and was made on a shoestring budget in what was doubtless a tight shooting schedule. Curiously, however, *Al Capone* is one of those pictures that seems oddly enhanced by its economical production values, as the greyish, bland, almost television-like photography, the inexpensive sets (which have a kind of built-in dinginess that makes them all the more effective) and a loud, blaring musical score that could have easily been used several years later for an episode of TV's "The Untouchables" all added to *Al Capone's* tough, realistic feel.

The film was especially well cast and, in addition to Steiger's, contained exceptional performances by Nehemiah Persoff, James Gregory, Martin Balsam and Joe De Santis in secondary roles. Persoff was superb as Johnny Torrio, the gangland chief who gives Capone his first job, and the scenery-chewing exchanges between Persoff and Steiger (both of whom were dedicated "method" actors) are especially enjoyable to watch. Fay Spain is at once vulnerable and sensuous as the woman who becomes Capone's mistress, and Mervyn Vye enjoyed several well-played vignettes as Capone's rival, Bugs Moran. The film also contained a particularly intense and realistic street fight, the unforgettable scene early in the story when Capone, working as a bouncer in a chintzy dockside bar, is forced to nearly murder with his

bare hands a drunken patron who refuses to leave quietly.

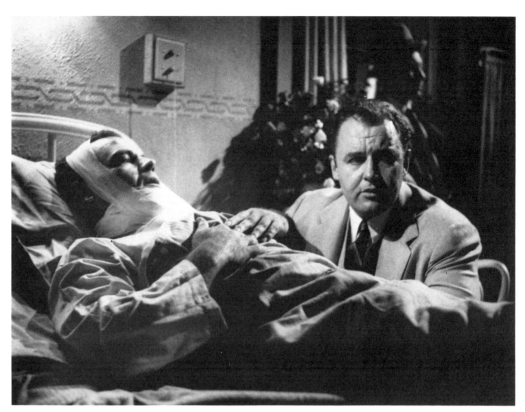

Nehemiah Persoff and Rod Steiger

Martin Balsam, Rod Steiger,
Nehemiah Persoff

213

SYNOPSIS

Al Capone (Steiger), a young hood with a fierce drive to make it to the top, is hired by his boyhood friend Johnny Torrio (Persoff), head of one of the most powerful gangs in Chicago. Working first as a bouncer, then as a bodyguard, Capone rises to become Torrio's "first lieutenant," persuading Johnny to let him kill "Big Jim" Colosimo (De Santis), the aging patriarch of Torrio's mob who, Capone believes, stands in the way of the gang's advancement. When Big Jim is eliminated, Capone and Johnny quickly become the virtual rulers of Chicago's criminal underworld, and they get rid of two of their biggest rivals, O'Banion and Weiss, in the process. When Johnny is seriously wounded in an assassination attempt sometime later, he decides to retire, leaving Capone to take charge of everything.

Capone, hungry to climb to even greater heights, starts a vast protection racket and becomes the number one gangster in Chicago. He falls in love with Maureen Flaherty (Fay Spain), the wife of one of his victims. Convinced by Capone that he had nothing to do with her husband's death, she becomes the gangster's mistress. The city's honest police chief (James Gregory) becomes appalled at Capone's grip on the town, and he vows to bring the criminal to justice one day. He actually succeeds in arresting Capone several times, but the corrupt legal system always allows the gangster to slip away. After returning from a vacation in Florida, however, Capone's luck gradually begins to fail him.

Maureen, discovering that Capone did, in fact, have her husband killed, leaves him . . . and one of the gangster's closest associates, a crooked newspaperman named Keely (Martin Balsam), betrays him to join a rival gang. As if this weren't enough, Capone is later arrested for income tax evasion, for which he is given a long stretch in Alcatraz. During his imprisonment there, Capone finds himself in almost daily contact with vengeful enemies and, on one particular afternoon, they gang up on him and nearly beat him to death. Several years later, Capone contracts an incurable illness and dies.

Al Capone's exploits were further explored in two later films—*The St. Valentine's Day Massacre* (1967), starring Jason Robards as the gangster, and the uncompromisingly bloody *Capone* (1975), in which Ben Gazzara essayed the role. Both of these were produced on a far more elaborate scale than the 1958 film and contained some fine acting from Robards and Gazzara, but the Rod Steiger version remains the definitive Capone picture.

THE ST. VALENTINE'S DAY MASSACRE

A 20TH CENTURY-FOX PICTURE.   1967

David Canary

George Segal and Jean Hale

CREDITS

Produced and directed by Roger Corman. *Screenplay by* Howard Browne. *Director of photography:* Milton Krasner. *Art direction:* Jack Martin Smith and Philip Jeffries. *Set decorations:* Walter M. Scott and Steven Potter. *Associate producer:* Paul Rapp. *Film editor:* William B. Murphy. *Unit production manager:* David Silver. *Assistant director:* Wes Berry. *Sound recording by* Herman Lewis and David Dockendorf. *Make-up by* Ben Nye. *Hair styles by* Margaret Donovan. *Filmed in* DeLuxe Color and Panavision. *Running time:* 99 minutes.

CAST

Al Capone: Jason Robards; *Peter Gusenberg:* George Segal; *Bugs Moran:* Ralph Meeker; *Myrtle:* Jean Hale; *Jack McGurn:* Clint Ritchie; *Sorello:* Frank Silvera; *Wienshank:* Joseph Campanella; *Scalisi:* Richard Bakalyan; *Frank Gusenberg:* David Canary; *May:* Bruce Dern; *Frank Nitti:* Harold J. Stone; *James Clark:* Kurt Krueger; *Fischetti:* Paul Richards; *Guzik:* Joseph Turkel; *Adam Heyer:* Milton Frome; *Schwimmer:* Mickey Deems; *O'Banion:* John Agar.

The St. Valentine's Day Massacre stands as one

216

of the best examples of how a truly opulant, large-scale gangster film can be made on a less than enormous budget. The picture, released in 1967, was produced and directed by Roger Corman, whose ability to make entertaining movies on even the most miniscule budget is well known. Throughout most of the fifties and sixties, Corman produced and directed an astonishing number of cheaply made horror, science-fiction and action pictures, many of which were quite good, and today Corman is generally regarded as one of the most skillful makers of "B" movies in history. The scores of films released during his boom period (with titles like *Attack of the Crab Monsters, Not of This Earth, Teen-age Caveman, She-Gods of Shark Reef, Wasp Woman* and *A Bucket of Blood*) never failed to turn a profit, and most of them have managed to garner a devoted cult following with the passage of time. In addition to his far-out horror fare, Corman also made several gangster films—*Machine Gun Kelly* (1958), *I, Mobster* (1959) and *Bloody Mama* (1970)—but none of them came close to the quality and style of *The St. Valentine's Day Massacre*.

Jean Hale and George Segal

Jean Hale and George Segal

Produced through 20th Century-Fox for around one and a half million dollars (some of which, according to Corman, was "overhead" and "studio costs"), the film was the most expensive the director had made to that time, though its budget was certainly not extravagant by late sixties standards. It is a credit to Corman's skill that he gave *The St. Valentine's Day Massacre* a rich, glossy look that belied its comparatively modest cost (in this respect, it was similar to the director's excellent Edgar Allan Poe films starring Vincent Price, which also had a big-budget "feel" even though they were produced with an eye toward economy). The cast was definitely first rate, featuring Jason Robards as Al Capone and Ralph Meeker as Bugs Moran, with George Segal, Joseph Campanella, David Canary, Bruce Dern, Frank Silvera, Harold J. Stone, Kurt Krueger, and Clint Ritchie filling out the major supporting roles.

The St. Valentine's Day Massacre is also of interest to film students because it features a pre-stardom Jack Nicholson in a bit part as one of the gangsters who helps set things up for the massacre. Nicholson appeared briefly in two scenes and had one line of dialogue that never fails to get a laugh whenever the picture is viewed today. As the killers hired to engineer the massacre load their machine guns, some of them are seen rubbing

George Segal
and Kurt Krueger

Ralph Meeker and Kurt Krueger

something onto the bullet tips. "What the hell are you doing?" one of the observers asks, to which Nicholson replies in a mock-serious, raspy "thug voice": "It's garlic. The bullets don't kill ya, ya die of blood poisoning." Though he lacked the physical resemblance to Capone that Rod Steiger had, Robards turned in a superb performance as the gangster, and was responsible for the film's most frightening moment . . . the chilling scene in which Capone prepares to kill two treacherous henchmen by bludgeoning them with a baseball bat.

SYNOPSIS

Chicago, the late twenties. Bugs Moran (Ralph Meeker), leader of the notorious North Side gang, begins muscling in on the bootlegging racket, which his rival, Al Capone (Robards), has dominated for years. With the aid of his chief hit man Peter Gusenberg (George Segal), Moran manages to take over twenty-eight speakeasys that were previously in Capone's control. Unable to tolerate this, Capone calls an emergency meeting of his gang, and orders the deaths of Moran and all who work for him.

Capone's resourceful lieutenant, Jack McGurn (Clint Ritchie), engineers an elaborate assassination plot to eliminate Moran and his mob all in one stroke. He hires a poor Italian immigrant, Sorello (Frank Silvera), to gain Moran's trust by selling the gangster a carload of high quality bootlegged whiskey. Pleased with the first shipment of liquor, Moran eagerly agrees to buy a second, only this time Sorello insists that Moran make the deal in person. Agreeing to Sorello's request, Moran designates that the next liquor deal will take place in an old garage in town, which is then carefully staked out by Capone's men.

A team of carefully chosen assassins is imported by Capone from the East and, on the morning of February 14, 1929, they raid Moran's garage dressed as policemen, killing Moran's entire gang in a blaze of machine gun fire. As it turns out, Moran escaped the slaughter after all, as he was unable to make it to the garage that morning due to some pressing personal matter.

As an interesting sidelight, Jack Nicholson was initially offered a major supporting role in the picture but declined it in favor of the bit. Because of the time and complexity involved in shooting the two scenes he was in, Nicholson actually stayed on the payroll longer, and was thus able to collect a heftier check.

George Segal

219

BONNIE AND CLYDE

A WARNER BROTHERS-SEVEN ARTS PICTURE.   1967

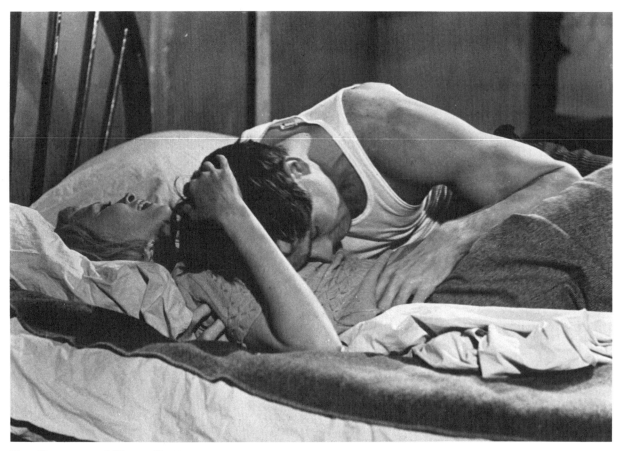

Faye Dunaway and Warren Beatty

CREDITS

Directed by Arthur Penn. *Produced by* Warren Beatty. *Screenplay by* David Newman and Robert Benton. *Director of photography:* Burnett Guffey. *Art direction:* Dean Tavoularis. *Film editor:* Dede Allen. *Sound recording by* Francis E. Stahl. *Set decorations:* Raymond Paul. *Special effects by* Danny Lee. *Music by* Charles Strouse. *Production manager:* Russ Saunders. *Script supervisor:* John Dutton. *Make-up by* Robert Jiras. *Filmed in* Technicolor. *Running time:* 111 minutes.

CAST

Clyde Barrow: Warren Beatty; *Bonnie Parker:* Faye Dunaway; *C. W. Moss:* Michael J. Pollard; *Buck Barrow:* Gene Hackman; *Blanche:* Estelle Parsons; *Frank Hamer:* Denver Pyle; *Ivan Moss:* Dub Taylor; *Velma Davis:* Evans Evans; *Deputy:* Clyde Howdy; *Sheriff Smoot:* Ken Mayer; *Bonnie's Mother:* Mabel Cavitt; *Bank Guard:* Russ Marker; *Farmer:* Joe Spratt; *Bank Customer:* Martha Adcock; *Bank Customer:* Sadie French; *Man:* Roy Heard; *Butcher:* James Stivers; *Eugene:* Gene Wilder; *Sheriff:* J. J. Lemmon, Jr..

Depression-era bank robbers Bonnie Parker and Clyde Barrow have, perhaps, inspired more movies than any other real-life criminals, and there have been no less than a dozen motion pictures either recounting their adventures or featuring characters with obvious similarities to the infamous pair. Some of these films, like the cult favorites *Gun Crazy* (1949), *They Live By Night* (1949) and *Thieves Like Us* (1974), were top-quality efforts, featuring excellent casts and fine direction, while others were merely cheap "exploitation" pictures such as *The Bonnie Parker Story* (1958) and *Big Bad Mama* (1974). However, this classic 1967 film, produced by and starring Warren Beatty, looms miles above them all, and is today regarded as one of the truly innovative movies of the sixties as well as one of the best gangster pictures ever made.

Aside from its obvious qualities as a piece of commercial movie-making, *Bonnie and Clyde* broke new ground in its frank approach to sexual matters and in its no-holds-barred violence, which, in 1967, was certainly close to the most graphic ever to have appeared in a major motion picture. The famous "ballet of blood" ending, when the two criminals are machine-gunned to death by police, had an extraordinary impact on audiences, who had never seen anything like it before. The on-

Faye Dunaway and Warren Beatty

Warren Beatty and Faye Dunaway

screen deaths of Parker and Barrow, in which the viewer actually sees them being torn to pieces in a spray of bullets, their bodies writhing horribly as they are riddled by the seemingly endless barrage, was so realistic that it was (and still is) rather difficult to watch. It still ranks, arguably, as the most effectively staged scene of its kind, thanks to director Arthur Penn's brilliant use of camera angles and slow-motion, and the flawless techniques employed for the sequence by special effects wizard Danny Lee. Lee created the superb illusion of bullets impacting upon the bodies through the use of explosive "squibs," tiny devices wired to the actors' clothing and detonated on cue by remote control. Though this technique is used in almost all screen shootouts today, it was relatively new to audiences of 1967, who were understandably startled by the effect this innovative trick produced.

The performances in *Bonnie and Clyde* were exceptional, garnering Academy Award nominations for nearly all the principals and winning the coveted Oscar for Estelle Parsons, who appeared as the eccentric, high-strung wife of Clyde's brother Buck (played by Gene Hackman). The script by David Newman and Robert Benton was written in such a way as to elicit strong audience sympathy for the leading characters, making

Barrow and Parker seem almost heroic. This, combined with the attractiveness and charisma of Beatty and Dunaway triggered a Bonnie and Clyde craze that lasted for several months following the film's release, during which there was a resurgance of popularity in thirties fashions which, for a time, came to be known as the "Bonnie and Clyde look."

The picture, of course, was a box office blockbuster and the subject of almost uniformly rave critical notices. It was chosen as the premiere feature of the Montreal International Film Festival, making it the most highly honored gangster picture to that time.

SYNOPSIS

The story takes place in the southwest during the thirties, where an ambitious, small-time bank robber, Clyde Barrow (Beatty), meets pretty Bonnie Parker (Dunaway), a waitress who dreams of escaping her drab life. Their attraction for each other is instantaneous, and Bonnie, believing that

Faye Dunaway, Michael J. Pollard, Warren Beatty

Gene Hackman, Estelle Parsons, Warren Beatty, Faye Dunaway, Michael J. Pollard

223

Clyde may be the answer to her dreams, begins
following him everywhere. On a lark, they rob the
local variety store, after which they drive far out
into the country in a stolen automobile. Later,
Clyde gives Bonnie her own handgun, a large
police-style revolver, which she learns to use with
deadly skill. Teaming up with Clyde's brother
Buck (Hackman), his wife Blanche (Parsons) and
C. W. Moss (Michael J. Pollard), they commit a
series of robberies in which several of the victims
are killed, and soon the Barrow gang becomes the
nation's most wanted criminals.

Later the gang abducts the mild-mannered
Eugene Grizzard (Gene Wilder) and his new wife,
and take the young couple on a wild joyride
throughout the southwest, during which the
gangsters and the newlyweds become friends.
When Eugene mentions that he is an undertaker,
however, Bonnie, knowing that fate will eventually
close in on her and Clyde, suddenly panics at this
reminder of death and orders Eugene and his wife
out of the car.

The Barrow gang's next robbery attempt is a
disaster, during which Buck is seriously wounded
by police. As Clyde jams the accelerator in an
effort to get away, Buck and Blanche are thrown
from the car, and federal marshals, armed to the
teeth, close in on the two helpless criminals. They
take Blanche into custody, and watch as the
horribly wounded Buck bleeds to death.

Thinking it would be best to hide out for a
while, Bonnie and Clyde take refuge at the ranch
of C. W.'s father, Malcolm Moss (Dub Taylor), who
betrays them to the local police. When Bonnie and
Clyde venture into town, they are once again
ambushed by lawmen. They manage to temporarily elude the cops, but Bonnie is wounded when
the deputies fire at them. She recovers, however,
and later composes a poem about her life with
Clyde. Not long afterward, the two are shot and
killed by police on a deserted country road.

Dub Taylor was excellent as C. W.'s venal,
opportunistic father, as was Denver Pyle as a
country sheriff who has a minor run-in with
Bonnie and Clyde. There was also an enjoyable
cameo by the then unknown Gene Wilder, appearing as the milquetoast undertaker who is
kidnapped by the Barrow gang while on his
honeymoon.

Warren Beatty and Faye Dunaway

THE BROTHERHOOD

A PARAMOUNT PICTURE.   1969

Luther Adler and Kirk Douglas

CREDITS

A Brotherhood Company Production. Directed by Martin Ritt. *Produced by* Kirk Douglas. *Screenplay by* Lewis John Carlino. *Director of photography:* Boris Kaufman. *Film editor:* Frank Bracht. *Art direction:* Tambi Larson. *Musical score by* Lalo Schifrin. *Running time:* 96 minutes.

CAST

Frank Ginetta: Kirk Douglas; *Vince Ginetta:* Alex Cord; *Ida Ginetta:* Irene Papas; *Dominick Bertolo:* Luther Adler; *Emma Ginetta:* Susan Strasberg; *Jim Egan:* Murray Hamilton; *Don Peppino:* Eduardo Ciannelli; *Pietro Rizzi:* Joe De Santis; *Carmelo Ginetta:* Connie Scott; *Jake Rotherman:* Val Avery; *Cheech:* Val Bisoglio; *Sol Levin:* Alan Hewitt; *Vido:* Barry Primus; *Toto:* Michele Cimarosa.

One of the most overlooked and underrated of the great gangster films is Kirk Douglas's *The Brotherhood,* which the actor both starred in and produced. It was not especially successful at the time of its original release, and it has been almost completely overshadowed in film history by the more expensive and elaborate *Godfather* films of the early seventies. The picture deserves a better

226

Kirk Douglas

fate, however, and may yet attain cult status as audiences discover what a truly entertaining gem it is. The picture, one of the first of its kind, dealt with the inner workings of a Mafia family and the conflict of Douglas, its tradition-bound patriarch, and his younger brother (played by Alex Cord), who feels the mob should "change with the times" by exploring new and more modern fields of activity.

The picture was directed with style by Martin Ritt, and the screenplay by Lewis John Carlino was extremely well crafted, but the primary reason for *The Brotherhood*'s quality was the excellent performance by Douglas, who practically carried the picture single-handedly. The actor enjoyed a complete change of pace in this role, affecting an Italian accent (which was thoroughly convincing) and sporting a thick black mustache that really made him look the part. The character of Frank Ginetta required Douglas to run a veritable gamut of moods and emotions over the course of the story, and he was by turns coolly businesslike (during the many meetings with the other members of the "syndicate," finely played by veteran character actors like Luther Adler and Eduardo Ciannelli), hilariously comic (in the superbly

played bit in which the drunken Ginetta, in a romantic mood, tries in vain to get undressed so he can take his wife to bed) and frighteningly menacing (during the scene in which he takes the treacherous Adler, whom he is planning to murder, for a last ride). It was certainly Douglas's most challenging role in years, and remains one of his best and most skillfully crafted performances.

As a gangster picture, *The Brotherhood* admittedly doesn't measure up to the magnificent *Godfather* films; at a scant 96 minutes, it lacks their epic "feel." Despite this, however, it is a film of definite appeal, and deserves a special place in movie history because it was one of the first major American films to attempt a serious story about the Mafia. The film's flavor was enhanced by the truly offbeat musical score by Lalo Schifrin, dominated by folksy "twanging" melodies that were especially appropriate during the scenes showing Frank and his family enjoying an outdoor feast in their native Italy.

SYNOPSIS

Frank Ginetta (Douglas), a high-ranking Mafia kingpin, invites his ambitious younger brother Vince (Alex Cord) to join the rackets as soon as he graduates from college. The week after his gradua-

Alex Cord and Kirk Douglas

227

Luther Adler and Kirk Douglas

Kirk Douglas

tion, Vince becomes Frank's chief adviser and second-in-command, and things go smoothly until the two clash over the future directions organized crime should take. Vince believes that the syndicate should "keep up with the modern world" by moving into areas like corporate business, while Frank thinks they should remain only in areas they really know.

As a result of their differing views, Vince and Frank have a bitter falling out, and, later, Frank violently objects when Vince and the other "board members" propose a move that might lead to conflict with the federal government. Dominick Bertolo (Luther Adler), an older member of the clan, believes that Frank is behind the times and should be ousted. When Bertolo takes steps to carry this out, Don Peppino (Eduardo Ciannelli), a retired Mafia chieftan who is fiercely loyal to Frank, warns Ginetta that Dominick has become an adversary and should be watched. The old don

Kirk Douglas and Alex Cord

Connie Scott and Kirk Douglas

Kirk Douglas

also tells Frank that, many years before, Bertolo had caused the deaths of forty elder statesmen of the mob, one of whom was Frank's revered father.

Frank takes Dominick for a ride to an abandoned warehouse where, with the help of his loyal aide Pietro Rizzi (Joe De Santis), he binds the treacherous Bertolo in such a way that the aging gangster slowly strangles himself. As Bertolo dies an agonizing death, Frank solemnly recites the names of the men Dominick betrayed. Realizing there will be mob reprisal for his execution of Bertolo, Frank flees to Italy with his wife and daughter.

Luther Adler and Kirk Douglas

Kirk Douglas

For a short time, he lives a peaceful "retirement" in the country, but his idyll comes to an end when Vince arrives for a visit. Frank realizes that his younger brother has been assigned to kill him for Bertolo's murder and, knowing that there is no escape, becomes resigned to what must happen. He takes Vince to the almond grove they had played in as youngsters, and then gives his younger brother a shotgun that once belonged to their father. Frank gives Vince the Mafia "kiss of death," after which the younger man performs his duty by blasting Frank.

Interestingly enough, *The Brotherhood*'s failure to score at the box office made its studio, Paramount, initially reluctant to produce the film version of another Mafia story that was offered to the studio several years later, Mario Puzo's *The Godfather*.

232

Kirk Douglas and Alex Cord

ORDER NOW!
More Citadel Film Books

If you like this book, you'll love the other titles in the award-winning Citadel Film Series. From James Stewart to Moe Howard and The Three Stooges, Woody Allen to John Wayne, The Citadel Film Series is America's largest and oldest film book library.

With more than 150 titles--and more on the way!--Citadel Film Books make perfect gifts for a loved one, a friend, or best of all, yourself!

A complete listing of the Citadel Film Series appears below.
If you know what books you want, why not order now!
It's easy! Just call 1-800-447-BOOK and have your MasterCard or Visa ready.

STARS
Alan Ladd
Barbra Streisand: First Decade
Barbra Streisand: Second
  Decade
Bela Lugosi
Bette Davis
Boris Karloff
The Bowery Boys
Buster Keaton
Carole Lombard
Cary Grant
Charles Bronson
Charlie Chaplin
Clark Gable
Clint Eastwood
Curly
Dustin Hoffman
Edward G. Robinson
Elizabeth Taylor
Elvis Presley
Errol Flynn
Frank Sinatra
Gary Cooper
Gene Kelly
Gina Lollobrigida
Gloria Swanson
Gregory Peck
Greta Garbo
Henry Fonda
Humphrey Bogart
Ingrid Bergman
Jack Lemmon
Jack Nicholson
James Cagney
James Dean: Behind the Scene
Jane Fonda
Jeanette MacDonald & Nelson
  Eddy
Joan Crawford

John Wayne Films
John Wayne Reference Book
John Wayne Scrapbook
Judy Garland
Katharine Hepburn
Kirk Douglas
Laurel & Hardy
Lauren Bacall
Laurence Olivier
Mae West
Marilyn Monroe
Marlene Dietrich
Marlon Brando
Marx Brothers
Moe Howard & the Three
  Stooges
Norma Shearer
Olivia de Havilland
Orson Welles
Paul Newman
Peter Lorre
Rita Hayworth
Robert De Niro
Robert Redford
Sean Connery
Sexbomb: Jayne Mansfield
Shirley MacLaine
Shirley Temple
The Sinatra Scrapbook
Spencer Tracy
Steve McQueen
Three Stooges Scrapbook
Warren Beatty
W.C. Fields
William Holden
William Powell
A Wonderful Life: James Stewart
DIRECTORS
Alfred Hitchcock
Cecil B. DeMille

Federico Fellini
Frank Capra
John Ford
John Huston
Woody Allen
GENRE
Bad Guys
Black Hollywood
Black Hollywood: From 1970 to
  Today
Classic Gangster Films
Classics of the Horror Film
Divine Images: Jesus on Screen
Early Classics of Foreign Film
Great French Films
Great German Films
Great Romantic Films
Great Science Fiction Films
Harry Warren & the Hollywood
  Musical
Hispanic Hollywood: The Latins
  in Motion Pictures
The Hollywood Western
The Incredible World of 007
The Jewish Image in American
  Film
The Lavender Screen: The Gay
  and Lesbian Films
Martial Arts Movies
The Modern Horror Film
More Classics of the Horror Film
Movie Psychos & Madmen
Our Huckleberry Friend: Johnny
  Mercer
Second Feature: "B" Films
They Sang! They Danced! They
  Romanced!: Hollywood
  Musicals
Thrillers
The West That Never Was

Words and Shadows: Literature
  on the Screen
DECADE
Classics of the Silent Screen
Films of the Twenties
Films of the Thirties
More Films of the 30's
Films of the Forties
Films of the Fifties
Lost Films of the 50's
Films of the Sixties
Films of the Seventies
Films of the Eighties
SPECIAL INTEREST
America on the Rerun
Bugsy (Illustrated screenplay)
Comic Support
Dick Tracy
Favorite Families of TV
Film Flubs
Film Flubs: The Sequel
First Films
Forgotten Films to Remember
Hollywood Cheesecake
Hollywood's Hollywood
Howard Hughes in Hollywood
More Character People
The Nightmare Never Ends:
  Freddy Krueger & "A Night-
  mare on Elm Street"
The "Northern Exposure" Book
The "Quantum Leap" Book
Sex In the Movies
Sherlock Holmes
Son of Film Flubs
Those Glorious Glamour Years
Who Is That?: Familiar Faces and
  Forgotten Names
"You Ain't Heard Nothin' Yet!"

For a free full-color brochure describing the Citadel Film Series in depth, call 1-800-447-BOOK; or send your name and address to Citadel Film Books, Dept. 1467, 120 Enterprise Ave., Secaucus, NJ 07094.